Systems and Network Infrastructure Integration

Series Editor
Jean-Charles Pomerol

Systems and Network Infrastructure Integration

Design, Implementation,
Safety and Supervision

Saida Helali

WILEY

First published 2020 in Great Britain and the United States by ISTE Ltd and John Wiley & Sons, Inc.

ISTE Ltd
27-37 St George's Road
London SW19 4EU
UK

www.iste.co.uk

John Wiley & Sons, Inc.
111 River Street
Hoboken, NJ 07030
USA

www.wiley.com

Library of Congress Control Number: 2020938682

British Library Cataloguing-in-Publication Data
A CIP record for this book is available from the British Library
ISBN 978-1-78630-526-8

Contents

Preface

This book, a true independent learning tool intended principally for students of network and systems sectors, is a guide to understanding the various facets of a network and systems integration project by learning the underlying concepts and acquiring the skills necessary to implement such projects. It is aimed at helping students acquire technical skills stemming from the analysis of needs, the specification of infrastructure characteristics, the definition of the equipment and components of the resulting networks, and their incorporation into the construction of a complete high-performance infrastructure that will satisfy the needs of a client company. Moreover, the methodological and organizational skills needed to oversee this type of project in terms of various considerations such as cost and deadline are also necessary and will be furnished by this book. This book also addresses the concept of Green IT, in order to raise students' awareness of environmental issues before they begin their professional lives, so that they will take these issues into account during the deployment of IT infrastructures.

The ultimate objective of this book is to enable students to learn how to design and develop network infrastructures for medium-sized and large businesses, and, more specifically, how to analyze needs and subsequently translate them into the design of the topology of a network that is fit for purpose. How do we define need in terms of interconnection equipment? How do we put an optimized addressing scheme in place? How do we determine the technologies, tools and manufacturers best suited to create a high-quality, high-performance network that is highly secure and accessible while being eco-friendly and state-of-the-art at the same time?

This book is made up of nine chapters, set out in two complementary sections adapted for IT network technicians; specifically:

– A methodological and organizational section that will enable students to understand, from the first chapter, the concept of specifications, and how to decipher them and to acquire the knowledge needed to manage an IT project, that is, the corresponding approaches, methods and tools. Indeed, it is vital to plan every stage of the implementation of an IT solution, to be familiar with its principal actors, and to know how to develop an efficient communication plan with regard to deliverables requested, milestone dates, etc.

This section will also provide an overview of the basic concepts of simulation in Chapter 2, and will more specifically introduce the GNS3 tool for the prototyping and testing of IT infrastructures before their on-site deployment. The use of this type of software protects an IT infrastructure integration project team for disrupting the operation of the production network. In addition, GNS3 is highly prized for teaching purposes, particularly in the absence of network hardware.

This section will also present the aspects of the environmental impact of IT infrastructures, or Green IT, with the aim of introducing students to and increasing their awareness of this reduced energy consumption approach in all network infrastructure implementation projects.

– A technological section that will address the purely technical aspects of network infrastructures in an organically laid-out sequence based on the actual process of setup and implementation.

Chapter 4, which begins this section, gives a concise introduction to the main network services generally provided by IT infrastructures.

The design of these infrastructures is a vital stage in the process of their implementation, which is discussed in Chapter 5.

Chapter 6 is dedicated to the theme of security. Any infrastructure integration project must be sure to implement certain security mechanisms depending on the needs of the client company.

Chapter 7 focuses on virtualization and cloud computing, two interdependent paradigms that are omnipresent in every network infrastructure today.

Concepts dealing with the quality of service (QoS) and high availability increasingly demanded by modern IT infrastructures, in which the types of applications are extremely diverse and performance is more and more of a priority, are discussed in Chapter 8.

The final chapter is dedicated to the supervision of a network infrastructure and its various tools, with the objective of monitoring the infrastructure installed in order to mitigate and possibly prevent technical failures.

Each chapter ends with a mental map in the form of a visual summary of the main points of information discussed, in order to better structure them and facilitate their memorization.

Saida HELALI
June 2020

1

Introduction to Project Management

"A little impatience can ruin a great project."

Confucius

> – Understanding the basic principles of project management.
> – Learning the principal methods and tools of project management.
> – Understanding the usefulness of specifications and how to interpret them.

1.1. Introduction

Managing an IT project is similar to managing any type of project in general. According to Wysocki, a project is a sequence of unique, non-repetitive, complex and connected activities intended to achieve an objective. This must be done within both a specific time frame and a budget, and in compliance with a set of specifications.

An IT project (ITP) requires technical skills (programming, security, networks, architecture, etc.), as well as organizational and communication skills. The objective is to design a reliable, viable and satisfactory IT solution for a client, particularly in terms of agreeing upon deadlines, cost and quality. There are multiple aspects to a project:

– functional: responds to a need;

– technical: complies with clearly defined specifications and limitations;

– organizational: adheres to a predetermined mode of operation (roles, culture, function, resistance to change, etc.);

– temporal: complies with deadlines;

– economic: adheres to a budget.

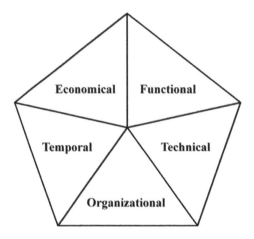

Figure 1.1. *Facets of a project*

1.2. Project management

Project management is an approach based on the application of knowledge, skills, tools, and techniques to project activities aimed at fulfilling the expectations of the parties involved in the project.

Every project can be broken down into phases. Each phase can be further broken down into stages, and these stages into tasks. The main phases of a project are shown in Figure 1.2.

Figure 1.2. *The main phases of a project*

– The initiation phase consists of defining the work to be carried out. It recalls its genesis, usefulness and end goal in answering "why" and "what" questions. The expected completion date can be set during this phase, and an overall budget can be estimated. A set of specifications must be drawn up at this point.

– The design phase involves the actual definition of the project; it structures, organizes and plans it. Its objective is to prepare and organize the implementation of the elements laid out during the initiation phase.

– The execution phase represents the realization or implementation of the project. Each of the points laid out in the action plan is worked on during this phase, according to the set of specifications.

– The closure phase involves building on recent experience with the goal of ongoing improvement through assessment reports and rigorous documentation.

1.3. Project management methods and tools

Project management methodologies enable a project to succeed and comply with the deadlines, budget and resources provided. They help each stage of the project to be completed, from planning to implementation, in the interests of efficiency and profitability.

Principal methodologies include:

a. Classic methods: these methods are most often used in project management. They are referred to as "cascading" because each stage must end by moving on to the next. The major disadvantage of this approach lies in its lack of flexibility with regard to changes.

b. Agile methods: these methods are gaining more and more popularity. They offer more flexibility and control in project management and better fulfill client expectations. Client needs are the cornerstone of agile methods. The client is involved throughout the entire project, which is executed according to an iterative, incremental process. Scrum, the agile method most often used, introduces the concept of sprints, which represent the different stages of the project. Throughout the project, existing functionalities will be continuously improved. It is also possible to add new functionalities if needed. Scrum is based on three roles:

– the product owner, who sets the technical requirements for the product,

– the development team, which develops the project according to the needs specified by the product owner and the scrum master,

– the scrum master, who oversees the realization of these objectives and is responsible for management within the project team. Successful communication with the product owner and the development team lies within the remit of the scrum master.

c. Adaptive methods: these methods adjust themselves to fit variations in projects, especially those that are complex and difficult to manage with a classic approach.

d. Critical path method: this method corresponds to the full set of tasks that must be accomplished in order to complete the project by a predetermined date. These critical tasks must not be subjected to any delay, otherwise the project will fall behind schedule.

e. The PERT method: this method is used to manage sequencing in a project. It involves representing the project in the form of a graph, a network of tasks whose sequencing will enable the achievement of preset objectives.

All of the tasks necessary for the execution of the project are listed and put in a specific order, with their dependence on one another established.

In this method, the stages of a project are represented graphically in a PERT diagram, which establishes the critical path that determines the minimum duration of the project.

f. The PRINCE2 (PRojects IN Controlled Environments, version 2) method: this method is a structured, pragmatic and adaptable project management methodology that can be used for any type of project. It guarantees that projects will be delivered on time, within budget and ensuring risk, advantage and quality management.

g. The Lean Management method: this method is used to provide high-quality work with minimal money, resources and time.

A wide range of tools is available for the management of a project. These are used to increase productivity and efficiency. Thus, it is necessary to know which ones to choose depending on our needs.

Table 1.1 recaps the main tools available for each phase of a project.

	Initiation (pre-project)	Design	Execution	Closure
Examples of tools	Objective tree RACI matrix Specifications	Pareto WBS Gantt diagram Communication plan Risk management	Collaborative work tools Brainstorming Problem-solving tools Control panel	Project review

Table 1.1. *Main tools for project management*

1.3.1. *Gantt diagram*

This is an effective and practical tool for project management created by Henry Gantt in 1917, which remains the most widely used representation tool. It consists of a graphic diagram useful for project planning and gives information and time frames for a project's phases, activities, tasks and resources.

Tasks are put in rows and durations (days, weeks or months) in columns. They are represented by bars whose length is proportional to the estimated duration. These can take place sequentially or partially or entirely simultaneously.

1.3.2. *RACI (Responsible, Accountable, Consulted, Informed) matrix*

The success of a project relies on the clear and precise definition of the roles and responsibilities of each actor involved. To do this, a RACI matrix is used. In this matrix, activities are laid out in rows and roles in columns. In each cell of the table, the role's responsibility for the activity is indicated, using the letters R, A, C or I.

	Role 1	**Role 2**	**...**	**Role m**
Activity 1	R	A	I	C
Activity 2	I	R	I	A
...	A	R	C	I
Activity n	C	R	C	I

Table 1.2. *Example of a RACI matrix*

It can be used to set out responsibilities in a project or within a company or business.

1.3.3. *The concept of specifications*

This is a contractual document describing what is expected from the project manager by the contracting authority. It is generally developed by the client and contains the following main sections: context, objectives, vocabulary or terminology, scope, schedule, etc.

The contracting authority is the party responsible for the expression of needs; they are the entity that places the order. The project manager is responsible for making these needs a reality.

The specifications must set out needs in a functional manner, independent of any technical solution with the exception of specifying the technical environment into which the solution requested must be inserted.

According to norm NF X 50-150 developed by the AFNOR, a functional specification document (FSD) is the document by means of which the requesting party expresses its needs in terms of service features and limitations. For each function and limitation, assessment criteria and their levels are defined.

NOTE.– The FSD is concerned with the service features of a product and their corresponding limitations, and does not contain any technical ideas or impose any solutions. Its objective is to propose the product best suited to provide the service(s) requested under the conditions specified and at minimal cost.

Knowing how to read and correctly interpret a set of specifications is very important for the success of the associated project. The project team must analyze needs, including understanding the expectations of the final users (the WHAT), and know how to put them into practice (the HOW). The team must gain a perfect understanding of the associated issue by asking itself the following questions:

– Who is requesting this solution?

– Who will use the proposed solution? With what benefits?

– What will be the solution's environment?

– What are the limitations and problems that may be encountered?

The ultimate goal always remains the satisfaction of the end-users' and clients' needs. These needs can be explicit or clearly stated, implicit or unstated but necessary. In this context, we can speak about functional specifications, pertaining to the functionalities expected of the project, and non-functional specifications, which represent the secondary characteristics to be offered.

Interpreting a set of specifications consists of:

– describing the project, including the context of work, motivations and objectives that will be evaluated at the end of the project, the challenges or difficulties to be overcome, and the criteria for success, or how to evaluate the project in relation to objectives;

– subsequently defining the phases of implementation of the project and the links between these phases using a Gantt diagram, for example. In addition, milestone targets and deliverables corresponding to each phase must be set, and a clear idea of the procedures has to be followed for the management and follow-up of the project.

1.4. Chapter summary

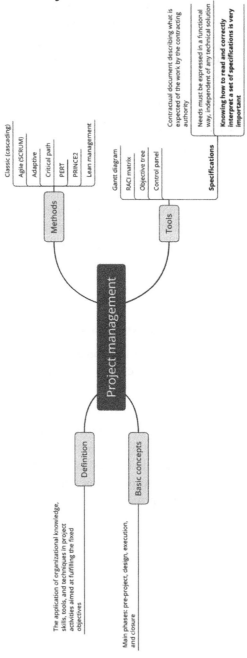

This chart is also available at www.iste.co.uk/helali/systems.zip

2

Simulating Network Architectures with GNS3

"Problems in school are like problems in life, but without their consequences."

Olivier Reboul

> – Understanding the concept of simulation and its main theoretical aspects, as well as its capabilities and limitations.
>
> – Understanding the main network simulation tools.
>
> – Understanding how to use the GNS3 supervision tool and its features to model a network infrastructure based on specific needs.

2.1. Introduction

As with the development of applications, system and network infrastructures, even simple ones, must be tested before they are put into production. This good practice is vital to avoid numerous errors during the production phase.

Simulating and testing network infrastructure projects before deploying them concretely saves time and money, and ensures that they will function properly. A network simulator is a software program, free or paid, which is used to create virtual representations of IT networks.

2.2. Definition

According to Wikipedia, network simulation is a technique by which a software program (simulator) models the behavior of a network, either using mathematical formulas to calculate the interaction between the parts of the network, or by recording and reproducing observations made of a real network.

Simulation is a fictional representation of reality. It means to imitate a situation. The best-known example is probably that of flight simulators, which enable pilots to train without risk.

In the context of networks, simulation refers to the reproduction of the architecture of a network without using any physical equipment. The interest of the simulation lies in its ability to test the features and operation of a network architecture at no cost and without hindering the normal operation of the production network.

To do this, the simulation uses a software program that calculates (we will also use the term "modeling" to refer to this process) and thus predicts the events that will be led to happen, taking their features into account. There are many free and paid tools to conduct these simulations, including GNS3, Cisco Packet Tracer, Cisco VIRL, Marionnet, Boson network simulator, Eve, etc.

A simulator can perform tasks to summarize the behavior of a network and its components, while an emulator can copy a network's behavior in order to stand in for it operationally.

Network simulators enable an architect or network engineer to build and assess an experimental model of a network, including its topology and application flow, bearing in mind that the network itself is being implemented in the real world.

In addition, network emulators enable architects, engineers and network engineers to precisely assess the reactivity, output and quality of an application before making changes or additions to a system.

Emulation is the ability to substitute something for the real object, while simulation has more to do with modeling the internal state of a target.

2.3. Introduction to GNS3

GNS3 (Graphical Network Simulator-3) is a graphical network emulator that is free to use, open source and reliable. It can also be used to test all types of equipment, not only that of one manufacturer in particular. Thus, it can be used to test CISCO, Juniper, SOPHOS, Citrix and many others. It is also multiplatform and can be installed on Windows, Linux and Mac operating systems. It uses a framework of open-source programs, each of which can emulate specific platforms to execute software programs corresponding to a provider. It is used to test configurations that will be deployed in the future on real equipment.

GNS3 is a network emulation tool similar to the Cisco tool PacketTracer, which is used to simulate a network infrastructure based on Cisco equipment and to configure equipment in order to reproduce the real infrastructure as closely as possible. GNS3 makes it possible to emulate networks more realistically, through both its ability to import real Cisco (or other) IOS into the routers emulated, and its ability to include in our virtual network real virtual hosts created with VirtualBox or other virtualization software. Thus, with GNS3, we can link the real to the virtual.

It includes the following components:

– Dynamips: emulates Cisco (or other) routers and switches and provides the corresponding environments or IOS;

– Dynagen: represents the Dynamips control and management software layer;

– Qemu: an emulator that enables GNS3 to execute Cisco ASA, PIX;

– VirtualBox or VMware: used to create and run virtual machines linked to Windows and Linux operating systems.

GNS3 is based on three concepts: simulation, emulation and virtualization. Since we have already discussed the concept of simulation, we will now introduce the other two concepts.

Emulation does not allow modeling, but actually identically reproduces the behavior of a software program and its hardware architecture. Virtualization uses the architecture of the host system, while emulation reproduces its software, which makes the virtualization perform more efficiently.

2.3.1. *Functionalities of GNS3*

– Simulates the behavior of two network interfaces connected via an Ethernet cable.

– Emulates routers, switches and other computers or servers. The respective components are operated with real software. Consequently, each virtual router requires a real IOS image. The thousands of lines of code of the highest-performance routers will be executed exactly as they would be in the real world, thus yielding the same behaviors as in production.

– GNS3 can be used to capture traffic between two virtual routers via Wireshark.

– It is possible to integrate virtualized Windows and Linux operating systems via VirtualBox or other virtualization solutions.

– GNS3 provides a link between the simulated network and the real physical network so that the virtual and physical components function together.

2.3.2. *Limitations*

GNS3 only works with specific types of routers. The IOS must be compatible with these types of routers. An IOS image cannot be used for a 2,800 router on a platform emulated for a 3,725. Moreover, GNS3 does not currently work with switch platforms. Generic switches can be integrated to simulate basic switching functions.

2.3.3. *GNS3 installation*

GNS3 exists for Windows, Linux and Mac, and can be downloaded from https://www.gns3.com/. You must create an account in order to download GNS3 for free.

You should follow the recommendations pertaining to the hardware configuration of your system. The minimal configuration is made up of a two-core processor, 4 GB of RAM and 1 GB of hard disk space for installation.

Only a few tests can be carried out with this configuration, due to lack of resources. The more powerful the system configuration, the more new routers, switches and other virtual servers can be added, and the larger the scale of the tests that can be conducted.

GNS3 uses well-known software programs from the systems and network sphere as components, some of which are required, including WinPcap, Wireshark, Dynamips, VPCS, and other optional programs such as SolarwindsResponse and Virtviewer.

2.3.4. *Getting started with GNS3*

Once installation is complete, we must first create a new project.

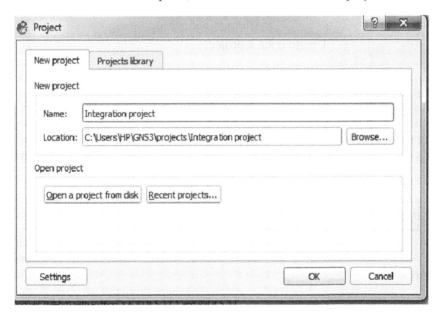

Figure 2.1. *Creation of a new project. For a color version of the figure, see www.iste.co.uk/helali/systems.zip*

When the project is created, the main window with various toolbars appears.

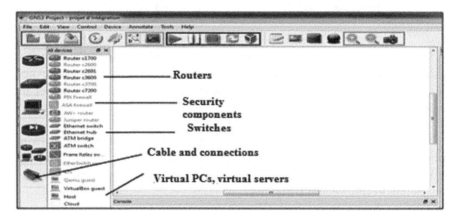

Figure 2.2. *Description of GNS3 interface. For a color version of the figure, see www.iste.co.uk/helali/systems.zip*

The outlined parts of Figure 2.2 are defined below.

Create/open a project

The first button allows you to connect with one click to the consoles of each device in the model. The second displays the configuration terminal of a router or a switch.

– The first button is the Start button, which launches the model's hardware.

– The second button pauses it.

– The third button turns it off.

– The fourth button restarts the whole thing.

– The fifth button displays the client's virtual machine.

The first two buttons are used to zoom (this can be useful when working with a large model).

The third button takes a snapshot of the model (to send to the client, for example).

2.3.4.1. *Integration of IOS images*

Using peripheral device selection, we can select a router and drag it toward the main window; however, this only works for previously configured equipment.

To do this, we first go to the menu bar in EDIT | IOS IMAGES AND HYPERVISORS to add the IOS images we have obtained (paid or free).

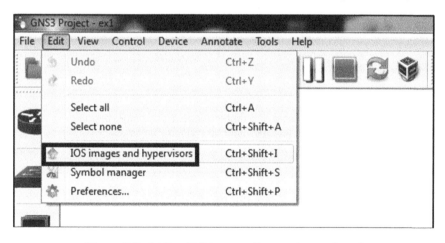

Figure 2.3. *Adding IOS images. For a color version of the figure, see www.iste.co.uk/helali/systems.zip*

We select the image file as well as the corresponding platform and model before saving.

A base configuration is saved as a text file (baseconfig.txt) that is automatically created in the specified path. This text file is later used to customize the base configuration of all routers according to the need.

The Cisco 1700 router is added and the following message appears: "Warning: IDLE PC will have to be configured!"

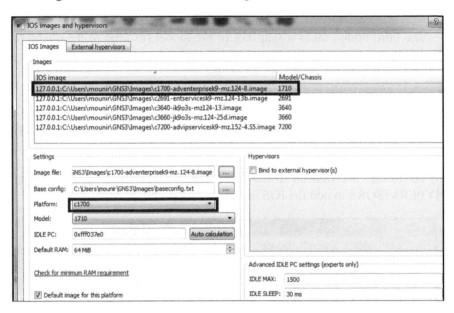

Figure 2.4. *Example of a router image. For a color version of the figure, see www.iste.co.uk/helali/systems.zip*

IDLE PC

The field "**IDLE PC**" is a value that enables the optimization of CPU resource allocation.

GNS3 consumes a very large amount of resources. Without additional configuration, a single router in GNS3 can use 100% of the processor. However, it is possible to reduce this drain on resources by defining an IDLE PC value. To do this, right-click on the router and then click the Start button. Next, right-click again and select IDLE PC.

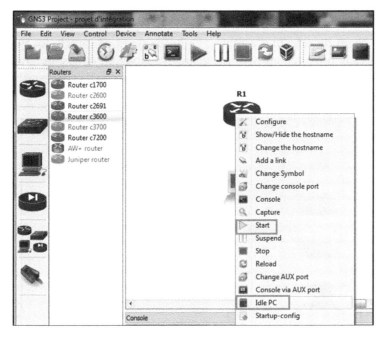

Figure 2.5. *Using the IDLE PC function. For a color version of the figure, see www.iste.co.uk/helali/systems.zip*

GNS3 calculates the possible values for IDLE PC and offers a range of choices, as shown in Figure 2.6.

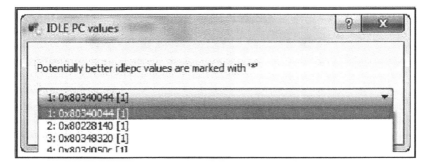

Figure 2.6. *Suggested range of IDLE PC values. For a color version of the figure, see www.iste.co.uk/helali/systems.zip*

Using the Task Manager, we can test the extent to which applying the suggested IDLE PC value will affect the processor load.

2.3.4.2. *Constructing a simple network topology*

We begin by selecting a router. Only the types of routers for which we have already provided an IOS image are available; all others are grayed out. In Figure 2.7, we have two router models available (the previously added C1700 and the existing C3600).

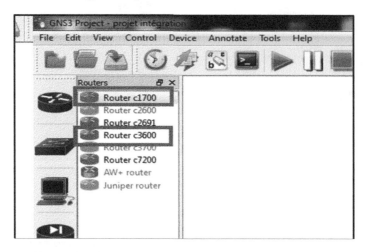

Figure 2.7. *Available router images. For a color version of the figure, see www.iste.co.uk/helali/systems.zip*

Using Drag & Drop, we drag the desired routers into the main window.

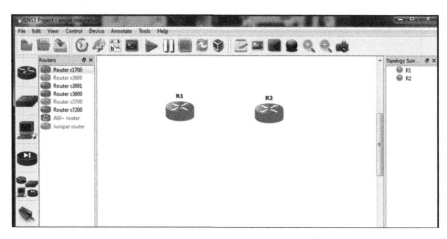

Figure 2.8. *Adding routers to a topology. For a color version of the figure, see www.iste.co.uk/helali/systems.zip*

To configure a router, right-click and select CONFIGURE.

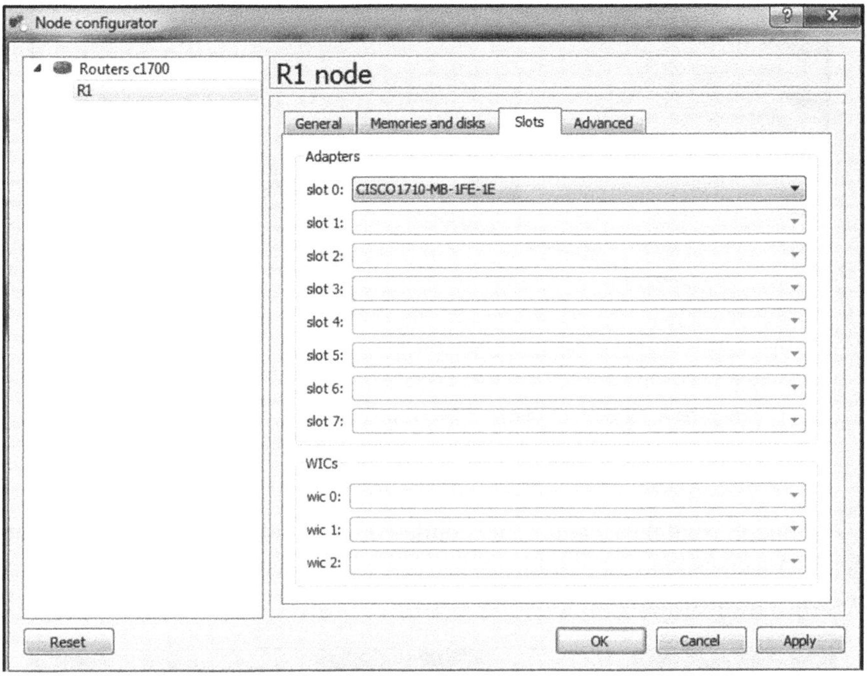

Figure 2.9. *Configuration of a router. For a color version of the figure, see www.iste.co.uk/helali/systems.zip*

Memory values can be adjusted here and, depending on the type, different modular locations can also be added.

GNS3 offers a selection of modules that can be virtually installed in routers.

To connect the two routers, simply select the type of corresponding connection using the left-hand button (a serial connection in this case) and click on the respective routers on the left to select the desired interface.

A corresponding connection line appears at R1, which is then dragged toward the partner router R2.

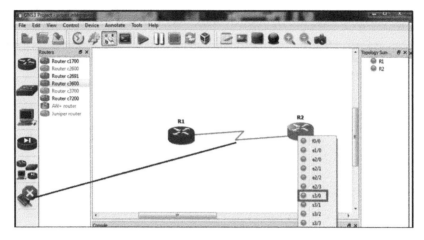

Figure 2.10. *Connection of two routers. For a color version of the figure, see www.iste.co.uk/helali/systems.zip*

Although switches cannot be emulated, it is still possible to simulate them. A corresponding button to the left allows you to select the desired switch. This is usually an Ethernet switch.

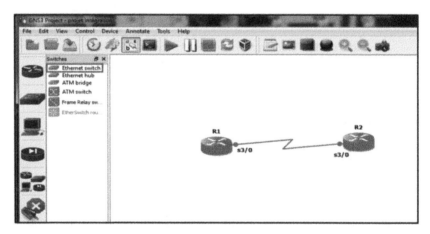

Figure 2.11. *Adding a switch. For a color version of the figure, see www.iste.co.uk/helali/systems.zip*

Peripheral devices are connected to the switch by selecting the Ethernet connection using the connection button on the left (as previously shown for the serial connection).

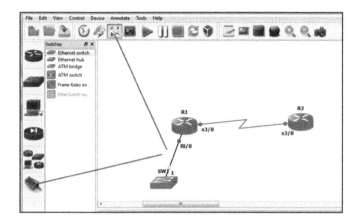

Figure 2.12. *Connection to a switch. For a color version of the figure, see www.iste.co.uk/helali/systems.zip*

Switches can be configured in a very generic way. To do this, we click on the switch to the right and select CONFIGURE. Now we can specify the VLAN and the mode assigned to each port.

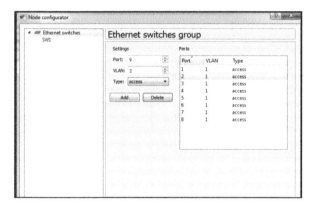

Figure 2.13. *Switch configuration. For a color version of the figure, see www.iste.co.uk/helali/systems.zip*

This allows us to control at least the basic aspects of a switch's configuration.

2.3.4.3. *Configuring a router*

Once a network infrastructure has been constructed, we move on to its configuration.

To access the router, simply double-click on it or right-click and select console. The standard console access program will open. Now we can configure the router exactly how we do with physical systems.

2.3.4.4. *Adding virtual systems*

It is possible to import virtual machines into GNS3, like an IOS image, or to use the cloud.

Method 1 (cloud)

Based on VirtualBox, VMware or any other virtualization software program installed on the host system executing GNS3, we can create GNS3 interfaces on our virtual machines and integrate them into GNS3.

To do this, we have to choose the host-only network interface in the virtualization software, illustrated by VMware Workstation shown in Figure 2.14, for example.

Figure 2.14. *Network configuration of a virtual machine. For a color version of the figure, see www.iste.co.uk/helali/systems.zip*

Next, we create a cloud connection in GNS3 via the End Devices button.

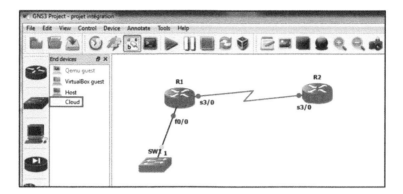

Figure 2.15. *Creation of a cloud connection. For a color version of the figure, see www.iste.co.uk/helali/systems.zip*

Before we can connect to the cloud, we must right-click on the cloud and select Configure, then choose the interface to connect to GNS3 (in this case VMnet1).

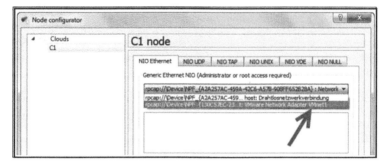

Figure 2.16. *Configuring the cloud. For a color version of the figure, see www.iste.co.uk/helali/systems.zip*

After selecting it, we click on Add to add this interface.

Now, we can connect the cloud to other objects, such as the switch, in the usual way.

Through this VMnet1 interface connection, each virtual machine (VM) connected via VMnet1 is integrated into GNS3.

Using the same principle, we can integrate the physical environment using the physical interface of our host computer as a cloud interface.

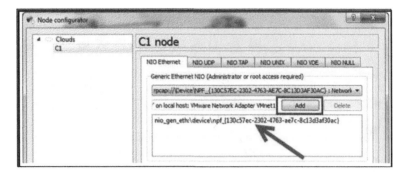

Figure 2.17. *Adding the interface. For a color version of the figure, see www.iste.co.uk/helali/systems.zip*

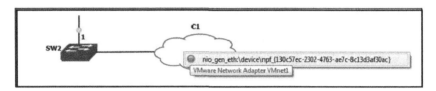

Figure 2.18. *Connecting the cloud with the switch. For a color version of the figure, see www.iste.co.uk/helali/systems.zip*

Method 2

A ready-to-use virtual machine is available, for which we will modify the network parameters. We choose the adapter2 card, for example, and put it into "Host-only Adapter".

Once the virtual machine is configured, we will prepare GNS3 to integrate this machine. To do this, we start the software program and go to "Edit", then to "Preferences", and finally to the "VirtualBox" menu.

We are particularly interested in the "VirtualBoxGuest" tab, where the virtual machine will actually be imported into GNS3. The first thing to do is to click on "Refresh VM List" so that the GNS3 native module will display the available virtual machines. These will then be available in the "VM List".

Finally, we can click and drag the "Virtual Guest" icon. The name of our VirtualBox machine should then appear in our topology. Then, we simply start it via GNS3 by right-clicking on Start.

2.4. Chapter summary

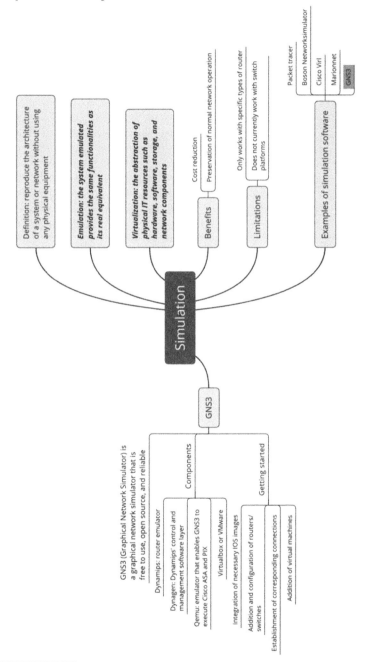

This chart is also available at www.iste.co.uk/helali/systems.zip

3

Green IT

"It's the duty of mankind to be nature's guardian, not its owner."

Philippe Saint-Marc

– Understanding the concept of Green IT and its challenges.

– Understanding the mechanisms and technical solutions for the implementation of a Green IT infrastructure.

– Describing and analyzing current mechanisms to reduce the energy consumption of IT products, particularly in data centers.

3.1. Introduction

When speaking of Green IT, it is vital to discuss the overall concept, that is, sustainable development.

This concept, introduced in the 1950s, took shape on June 16, 1972, in Stockholm, as part of the adoption of the Declaration of the United Nations Conference on the Human Environment, and then in 1987 as part of the Brundtland report published by the UN:

A development that meets the needs of the present without compromising the ability of future generations to meet their own needs. It contains within it two key concepts: the concept of "needs", in particular the essential needs of the world's poor, to which overriding priority should be given; and the idea of limitations imposed by the state of technology and social organization on the environment's ability to meet present and future needs.

(Brundtland report)

Sustainable development relies on three cornerstones: economy, social issues and ecology.

In 2012, the *Agence Française de Normalisation* (AFNOR), or French Standardization Organization, defined a state as "sustainable" "if the components of the ecosystem and their functions are preserved for present and future generations. The components of the ecosystem include, besides human beings and their physical environment, plants and animals. For human beings, the concept implies a state of equilibrium in the satisfaction of basic needs: the economic, environmental, social, and cultural conditions of existence within a society".

Sustainable development is therefore becoming a key part of businesses' strategy. Their enthusiasm for Green IT is dictated, on the one hand, by a public that is paying much closer attention to businesses' commitment to environmental and social issues (brand image), and, on the other hand, by shareholders demanding accountability on the part of the company with regard to matters of social responsibility.

ICTs (information and communications technologies) represent both a risk and an opportunity for sustainable development. They are problematic because they undeniably have negative environmental impacts, but paradoxically offer opportunities to reduce the ecological impacts of other human activities.

3.2. Introduction of concept

Green IT, or Eco-ICT, or *informatique verte* in French, is a concept defined as all information and communications technologies designed so that their economic, ecological and social footprints are optimized. Their objective is to help humanity to achieve its sustainable development goals.

"Information and communications ecotechnologies" are information and communications technologies whose design or use help to reduce the negative effects of human activity on the environment. They are aimed at reducing energy consumption and greenhouse gas emissions (French official journal, July 12, 2009).

The Rio+20 conference held in 2012 recognized "the essential role played by ICT and broadband networks as enablers of sustainable development".

3.3. Green IT trigger factors

Information technology generates a significant quantity of toxic electrical and electronic equipment waste (EEEW), or e-waste, such as computers, printers, digital cameras and mobile telephones. This waste is harmful to both the health of human beings and the environment.

In 2014, the United States and China produced one-third of the world's electronic waste, which according to the UN totaled 41.8 million tons, compared to 39.8 million tons in 2013. In 2016, the quantity of e-waste reached 44.7 million tons, with 50 million tons projected by the UN in 2018.

ICTs produce as much CO_2 as civil aviation, or 2% of emissions linked to human activity (Gartner, 2007).

ICTs, whether hardware or software, consume large amounts of energy, water and metal, thus constituting a drain on natural resources, and they generate a significant quantity of dangerous waste that pollutes the air, ground, etc., causing ecosystemic changes.

3.4. Benefits of Green IT

Eco-ICT, or Green IT, contributes to the reduction of the negative environmental impacts of the corresponding equipment, including their own ecological impacts, throughout their lifecycle (design, manufacture, use, recycling). Moreover, they also help to reduce indirect impacts stemming from other human activities.

There are two types of Eco-ICT: Green for IT (or Green IT 1.0) and IT for Green (or Green IT 2.0). Both of these categories seem to have the same objectives: optimizing energy efficiency and reducing the carbon footprint of businesses and their products and services, as well as researching ways to boost economic and social performance.

– Green IT 1.0 (or Green for IT) targets the ICT industry's eco-responsibility to reduce the ecological footprint of infrastructures, IT hardware and software. This translates concretely into the eco-design of products, the setting up of green data centers and the management of e-waste.

– Green IT 2.0 (or IT for Green) targets IT usages for other sectors. This includes the use of ICTs in other sectors in order to achieve the same goal of reducing the carbon footprint, as well as its associated costs. Examples of this IT usage vary greatly, ranging from telework, the intelligent organization of transport, and the construction of intelligent buildings and transportation.

The benefits of sustainable development can be summarized as:

– reduction of electrical energy consumption and greenhouse gases that are harmful to the environment;

– eco-design enabling the environmental dimension to be taken into account in every stage of the lifecycle of ICT technologies. Environmental assessment is based on lifecycle analysis (LCA) and includes a method that is internationally recognized as a powerful tool capable of calculating the impact generated by products throughout their lifecycle.

3.5. The lifecycle of ICTs

Each phase of the lifecycle requires energy and raw materials. Therefore, it is essential to refer to this lifecycle in order to analyze the environmental impacts of ICTs:

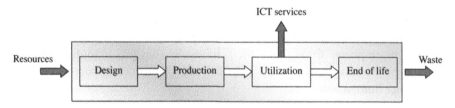

Figure 3.1. *Lifecycle of ICT equipment. For a color version of the figure, see www.iste.co.uk/helali/systems.zip*

– Design phase: the idea is to design a product while taking into account its environmental impacts throughout its lifecycle. Stresses linked to environmental impacts must be included in the design from the beginning. However, understanding of the product (structure, properties and performance) is limited, especially in the early part of the design phase; therefore, modeling of its lifecycle is carried out using a simplified LCA that consists of predicting the impact of a product in development based on its similarity to previous generations. Environmental stresses should be taken into account in the preliminary stages of the design phase.

– Production phase: ICT production generally requires a significant quantity of toxic materials, such as lead and mercury, as well as rare, non-renewable, expensive materials, such as copper, gold and silver. For example, 22% of the mercury produced worldwide each year is used in the manufacture of electrical and electronic products. This phase is the one during which small ICTs (PCs, telephones, etc.) consume the largest portion of the energy consumed during their lifecycle.

– Utilization phase: the utilization of a digital infrastructure consumes energy. 4G and 5G networks consume the largest portion of energy during this phase. For example, computers consume energy only during their use; web servers require non-stop energy consumption. Thus, for servers, efforts must be concentrated on the utilization phase, which is not the responsibility of the manufacturers of digital networks, but rather of the service providers and their clients.

– End-of-life phase: recycling constitutes a key point, as it is beneficial for the environment insofar as it enables the recovery of mineral resources. ICTs contain toxic materials that continue to generate a major social and environmental debate.

3.6. Mechanisms and technical solutions for the implementation of a Green IT infrastructure

More and more projects using a Green IT approach are being implemented, that is, projects whose objective or effect is to reduce the footprint of a product or service in economic, ecological and social terms. This reduction is achieved thanks to digital technologies. There are several themes at play: intelligent electrical networks (smart grids), intelligent transportation and transport, environmental and urban monitoring, virtualization, telework and teleconferencing, intelligent buildings, and eco-friendly software design.

Examples of improvement areas and solutions to make an IT system more eco-friendly that have been put forward include:

– the use of specific software programs that automate the functions of monitoring and shutdown of machines when they are not in use. This approach avoids waste linked to user activity;

– the virtualization of servers, which enables a better utilization rate of hardware platforms, and consequently a reduction in the number of servers. It also enables a reduction in the fleet of workstations by deploying light client-oriented architectures that consume 10 times less energy than a workstation;

– the optimization of climate control of operating centers and the implementation of high-performance cooling solutions;

– the use of heat emanations: some centers collect heat from central units and use it to heat their premises;

– the increased externalization of work and telework;

– the adoption of a data center design that is efficient in terms of energy consumption, cooling, server configuration, consolidation, cabling/wiring, redundancy, etc.;

– the measurement of the efficiency of existing data centers using current measurements such as power usage effectiveness (PUE), which measures energy efficiency. The monitoring of progress made with business intelligence tools is possible;

– datacenters and cloud computing enable the purchase of fewer new servers and the optimization of existing infrastructures. However, they consume large amounts of energy, especially for businesses with large infrastructures. One solution consists of optimizing energy efficiency or PUE. The latter is determined by dividing the data center's total electrical energy consumption by the quantity of energy actually used by the servers. For example, Google has achieved an average PUE of 1.2 by using high-performance cooling technologies;

– increasing users' awareness so that they will turn off their computers, print only when necessary and choose video conferencing over physical travel;

– the definition of a responsible purchasing policy for the acquisition of equipment adapted to needs, preferably reconditioned or, if this is not possible, new but designed to be eco-friendly and EPEAT, RoHS and/or ENERGY STAR certified. It is preferable to opt for equipment that can be repaired to maximize its lifecycle. In the case of a software purchase, this should be eco-developed and should have an operative lifespan designed to fit a given technological configuration;

– the controlling of data transport and storage by targeting e-mail recipients, cleanup of bulk e-mail lists, avoiding attachments or compressing them to limit their size, cleanup of archives, etc.

In addition, numerous and wide-ranging assessment indicators should be defined for the environmental footprint of business IT.

As we can see, the possibilities that exist with regard to IT ecology are numerous and sometimes conflict with one another. On the one hand, maximizing the lifecycle of computers avoids the consequences of disposing them, and, on the other hand, a new PC consumes less energy. The quest to attain a relatively fragile state of ecological equilibrium is an ongoing one.

3.7. Green IT labels and standards

– BLUE ANGEL: created in Germany in 1978, this independent eco-label is based on the criteria of recyclability and the reduction of pollution and energy consumption of computers, printers (especially those that consume toner) and mobile telephones.

– EPEAT (Electronic Product Environmental Assessment Tool): created in the United States in 1992, this independent eco-label takes into account the environmental effect throughout their lifecycles of computers, tablets, mobile telephones, printers and servers. It is based on 23 mandatory criteria and 28 discretionary criteria covering the entirety of a lifecycle. It is awarded in three forms: EPEAT bronze for compliance with the 23 mandatory criteria alone, EPEAT silver for compliance with all the mandatory criteria and at least 50% of the discretionary criteria, and EPEAT gold for meeting all the mandatory criteria and at least 75% of the discretionary criteria.

– RoHS (Restriction of Hazardous Substances in Electrical and Electronic Equipment): this is a European directive aimed at limiting the use of certain dangerous substances in electrical and electronic equipment, such as lead, mercury, cadmium and hexavalent chromium.

– TCO: created in Sweden in 1990, this independent eco-label uses the following criteria for computers, screens, printers and mobile telephones: ergonomics, electromagnetic emissions, energy consumption, manufacturer ISO 14001 certification, low noise, compliance with RoHS norms and recyclability of materials.

– IEEE 1680: this refers to an IEEE norm for environmental performance criteria for office computers, laptop computers and monitors.

– ISO 14000-1: this concerns environmental management intended to improve environmental performance while maintaining productivity.

– ENERGY STAR: an American label applicable to PCs, printers, photocopiers, fax machines, scanners, modems, etc., which possesses an automatic sleep or standby function characterized by reduced operating power.

3.8. Some examples of Eco-ICTs

– In 2011, one of Facebook's data centers proved to be full. The question at that point was whether it was necessary to build a new data center, bearing in mind the question of the ecological footprint. The solution chosen was to replace the language PHP with C, thus freeing up 50% of the space available in the existing data center. This choice allowed Facebook to save more than $100 million and to reduce its ecological footprint at the same time.

– Fairphone: this mobile telephone contains no rare metal mined in the areas of armed conflict. It is also manufactured in factories that comply with social criteria. It is fully repairable and part of a specific recycling plan.

– An eco-responsible data center at the University of Lille 1: the cool corridor solution bringing together all of the IT servers in the IT resource center has been adopted. This is a system that separates the flows of warm and cool air. The server rooms are organized into warm and cool corridors. Only the cool corridors are air-conditioned, that is, those faced by the front side of the arrays. This simple arrangement in itself reduces the need for heat dissipation. Moreover, it would be quite possible to equip the rooms with extractor fans installed above the warm corridors to vent the air and potentially redirect it, in order to heat offices, for example.

– The goal of the Green Code Lab is the worldwide promotion of the eco-design of software using a set of methodologies and good practice development. It bases its work on the principle of software eco-design, which enables businesses to integrate environmental impact criteria into an application or digital service from the design phase onward in order to reduce the impact throughout its lifecycle. These projects include the "green code label" for labeling an eco-designed website and the "Web Energy Archive", which is used to add an environmental rating to a website.

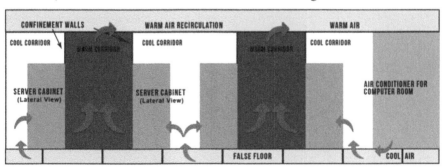

Figure 3.2. *Cool corridor solution. For a color version of the figure, see www.iste.co.uk/helali/systems.zip*

3.9. Chapter summary

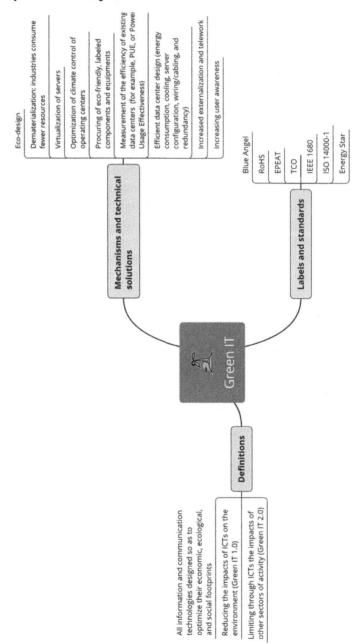

This chart is also available at www.iste.co.uk/helali/systems.zip

4

Design of Network Infrastructures

"Well begun is half done."

Aristotle

- Recalling the theoretical concepts related to IT networks.

- Describing the approaches, methods and models of network design.

- Understanding the hierarchical model and its three layers, as well as the way in which they are used in network design.

- Understanding the methodologies and models of Cisco network architecture design.

4.1. Introduction

The design of IT networks constitutes a vital stage in the implementation of an IT infrastructure. Meticulous design ensures proper functioning of the network environment as well as its possible growth.

In addition, design has become an arduous task as network environments become more and more complex, with diversified equipment and media, as well as interconnections with other external networks.

Therefore, it is imperative to take all of these aspects into account in order to design a stable, high-performance and upgradeable network infrastructure.

A successful design should be:

– functional: the network infrastructure must satisfy the requirements of the enterprise defined in the specifications and must enable users to carry out their work under the best possible conditions;

– upgradeable: the network to be designed must demonstrate the capacity for expansion. Consequently, designers must provide for the growth of the network infrastructure without being forced to make major changes to the initial design;

– adaptive: the design must be capable of integrating new technologies;

– easy to manage: from the design phase onward, mechanisms must be provided for to facilitate the management and monitoring of the network, in order to ensure its stable functioning.

The infrastructure designer must pay attention to performance indicators such as response time, speed of communication, cost and availability to set up efficient, optimized networks. To carry out these tasks properly, the designer must base his or her actions on the breakdown approach, since the more a task is divided, the easier the management becomes.

4.2. The founding principles of networks

4.2.1. Definition and preliminaries

A communications network is all of the hardware and software resources interconnected by a wired or wireless transmission system, thus ensuring the transmission and exchange of information between different entities. Networks are bound by certain norms and specifications depending on their architecture, geographical coverage, transmission speed and the nature of the information transmitted.

Depending on the type of information exchanged and the nature of the equipment involved, we differentiate the following types of networks:

– telephone networks: these networks are used to carry the voice between telephone sets. These are the oldest type of network (switched telephone network – STN, GSM);

– broadcasting networks: these networks broadcast television channels from television studios to private individuals (Eutelsat);

– digital data networks: these networks are designed to exchange digital data between IT equipment and to share IT resources (such as Frame Relay).

The current tendency is to combine these three types of networks into a single converged network that can be used to transmit any type of information. These new networks, also called next-generation networks (NGN), are becoming extremely popular.

In the following sections, we will focus particularly on digital data networks, which enable reductions in cost thanks to the sharing of hardware and software resources as well as the ease of communication.

4.2.2. Classification of digital data networks

Several criteria can be used to classify networks, such as operating mode, that is, client/server networks or peer-to-peer, nature of transmission support (wired or wireless), output, and size or distance of the network.

This last criterion is most widely used. There are PAN (Personal Area Networks), LAN (Local Area Networks), MAN (Metropolitan Area Networks) and WAN (Wide Area Networks).

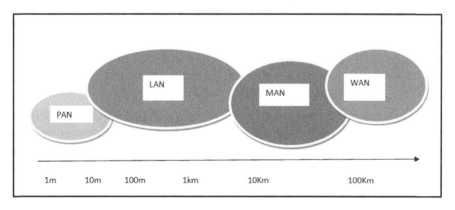

Figure 4.1. *Standard network classifications*

A digital data network is composed of a physical or hardware part and a logic or software part.

4.2.3. *Components of a network*

4.2.3.1. *Hardware part*

A network is composed of a set of equipment that can be classified as follows:

– Terminal equipment: this represents the hosts at the end of a communication and can be computers, workstations, servers, printers, etc.

– Transmission supports: they are coaxial cables, twisted pair cables, optical fibers, Hertzian beams, radio waves, etc.

– Interconnection equipment: they are hubs, switches, bridges, routers, gateways, etc.

- Routers: they are network layer hardware constituting one of the most powerful items of equipment in this layer. This equipment is used to interconnect different IP networks and to segment the local network into multiple single physical and logical networks. It is also used to interconnect remote networks such as the Internet and to transfer IP traffic using its routing table to dynamically determined correct destinations.

- Switches: they are layer 2 equipment that controls flow, as well as detects and corrects errors and reduces overload. Switches also determine the size of the areas of collision and diffusion. They use microsegmentation to reduce the size of the collision area, consequently improving network performance. They also enable the creation of virtual local area networks (VLANs) and broadcasting domains separated according to users' work groups.

They transfer traffic according to CAM destination addresses found in frames and the switching table (CAM table).

A multilayer switch is a switch capable of executing routing tasks and advanced services. It is also called an L3 switch.

- Bridges, hubs, repeaters: a bridge filters traffic between two physical segments according to MAC addresses. A hub concentrates connections and expands the physical segment. Unlike switches, traffic exits all of its ports; it does not make any decisions about the destination of this traffic and thus presents only a single collision domain. A repeater is a piece of equipment that simply regenerates a signal.

- Wi-Fi access points: they supply wireless service within a radio coverage area.

4.2.3.2. *Software part*

The data transmitted by terminal equipment via networks is transported in the form of a binary signal via a set of specific rules called communication protocols.

Protocols constitute a common language used by communicating parties to find one another, connect to each other and exchange information. They define a set of parameters related to a communication such as physical characteristics (modulation, physical support types, connector types) and types and formats of the messages exchanged.

By the early 1970s, each manufacturer had developed its own network solution around private architectures and protocols (SNA for IBM, DECnet for DEC, DSA for Bull, TCP/IP for the DoD, etc.).

Consequently, it was impossible to interconnect these different "proprietary" networks, and the installation of open – and thus interoperable – systems became necessary. Thus, an approach to standardize and define standard communications models was implemented by standardization organizations such as ISO, IUT, IEEE and IETF.

A communications model simplifies the process of communication between nodes, which can be highly heterogeneous in organizing communications in the form of a multilayer hull hierarchy. Each layer carries out a function specific to the communication and displays determined characteristics.

In addition, a communications model has multiple advantages: it enables a better understanding of the functioning of communications, encourages interoperability, simplifies the diagnostic and repair process, and allows the change or addition of functionalities to one layer without impacting the others.

The OSI model

The OSI (Open System Interconnection) model was developed by the ISO and is made up of seven layers, each illustrating a specific network function. It provides a reference architecture for exchanges between computers.

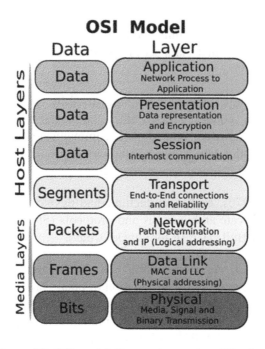

Figure 4.2. *OSI model. For a color version of the figure, see www.iste.co.uk/helali/systems.zip*

Functions of hardware layers

The physical, data link, network and transport layers are responsible for the transfer of data between the nodes of a network.

Layer	Role	Example of protocol
Transport	End-to-end data transfer	TCP
	Delivery in connected and non-connected mode	UDP
	Correction of errors before retransmission	

Network	Routing packets from the source toward the destination Ensuring local addressing to determine pathway	IP
Data link	Transfer of information between two pieces of equipment connected by a physical support Media access Physical addressing Error detection	HDLC Ethernet Token Ring Wi-Fi
Physical	Routing bits between pieces of equipment Specifying voltage, support and the type of connector	

Table 4.1. *Functions of hardware layers*

Functions of software layers

The session, presentation and application layers are responsible for managing applications.

Layer	Role	Example of the protocol
Application	User interface	HTTP, FTP
Presentation	Data representation Specific processing (compression, encryption)	ASCII EBCDIC JPEG
Session	Management of dialogue between users Separation of data from different applications	Operating system

Table 4.2. *Functions of software layers*

The TCP/IP model

TCP/IP was invented by the US Department of Defense (DoD), which was seeking a routable, robust and high-functioning protocol that could be used to create wide area networks able to function even in the event of nuclear war.

TCP/IP has become the standard model for interoperability between heterogeneous computers. This interoperability is one of the main assets of TCP/IP. The success of the TCP/IP model is due largely to its openness. Source codes developed independently of a specific architecture or a particular operating system are available at no cost.

Consequently, TCP/IP protocols do not rely on physical supports and can function on any type of platform. Indeed, TCP/IP can be transmitted by various types of supports, including a serial line, a coaxial Ethernet cable, a leased line, a token-ring network, a radio link, a laser ray link, infrared, ATM, fiber optic, etc.

The TCP/IP model is made up of four layers: application, transport, Internet and network access.

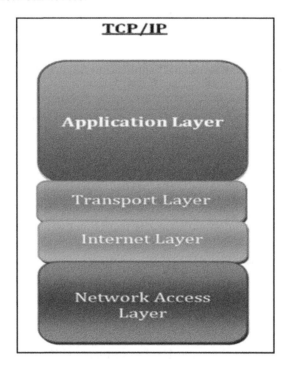

Figure 4.3. *TCP/IP model*

The role of each of the four layers is specified in Table 4.3.

Layer	Role
Application	File transfer, navigation
Transport	Control of data flow Acknowledgment
Internet	Logic addressing Routing
Network access	Physical interface with the network Error checking

Table 4.3. *Layers of the TCP/IP model*

The OSI and TCP/IP models are compared in Figure 4.4.

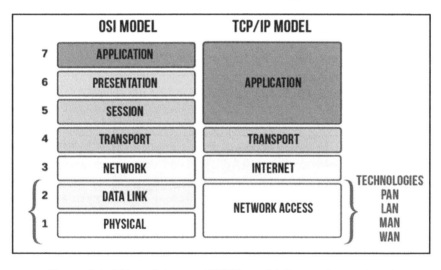

Figure 4.4. *OSI model versus TCP/IP model. For a color version of the figure, see www.iste.co.uk/helali/systems.zip*

4.2.4. *Measuring network performance*

There are three main indicators by which we judge the performance of a network: output, latency and packet loss. These yardsticks can be useful during the problem diagnostic process for an IT network, or to assess this network's performance, or during the design process:

– Output: the amount of data sent and received per unit of time.

– Latency: the time required to transport a packet via a network from a source to a destination. It is dependent on every part of the chain used to transport date: communicating stations and, more specifically, their network cards; LAN links with switches; WAN links with routers. It can be made up of the following:

- *Propagation time*: the time it takes for a bit to move from the transmitter to the receiver (or the time required for a packet to move from point A to point B). It is measured by the distance ratio separating A and B over the propagation speed of the signal.

- *Transmission time*: the time needed to release a message into the network (time required by a node [network equipment] to send the entire packet on the media).

- *Processing time*: the time required for intermediary and terminal equipment to process data during transmission.

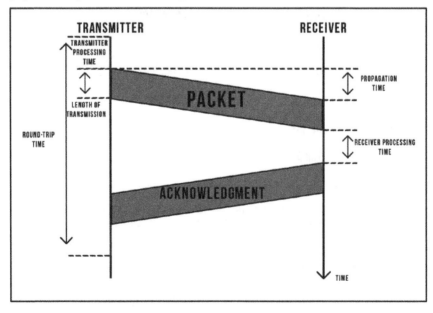

Figure 4.5. *Network delivery time*

Latency can be measured using the **ping** command:

Jitter: variation in latency. Packets arrive irregularly depending on the network load. It has an enormous influence on VoIP quality. If the jitter becomes important, the quality of the voice conversation (VoIP) will be severely affected.

– Packet loss: this is the number of packets lost per 100 packets transmitted by a host on the network. It has a significant effect on the quality of the link by requiring the retransmission of data.

4.2.5. *Concepts of collision domain/broadcast domain and VLANs*

The collision domain is the logic area of the network that generates frames that then collide. All shared-support environments dependent on concentrators are collision domains.

In a switched environment, each host connected to a switch port constitutes a dedicated connection and a separate collision domain.

A broadcast domain is a logic area that includes all peripheral devices receiving any broadcast packet sent by a network host.

Broadcast traffic is usually significant, which is generated, for example, by ARP and DHCP protocols. This traffic generally involves only a limited number of machines and is thus a source of binary output waste, increased latency and pointless consumption of calculation power.

To this is added the fact that today's users are more and more mobile, and their geographical location is not necessarily dependent on their logic membership. Now, employees relatively distant from one another can belong to the same broadcast domain.

In addition a broadcast domain's traffic is visible, thus creating problems with confidentiality.

Two approaches can be used to resolve the issues mentioned above.

The first approach, physical segmentation, is characterized by the creation of IP sub-networks interconnected via routers. The disadvantages of this option include a lack of upgradeability, increased cost and difficulty of maintenance.

The second approach involves logical segmentation, or virtual local area networks (VLANs). A VLAN is used to group users logically and to increase output, improve security, reduce costs, and facilitate mobility and management.

VLANs are configured via switches. One switch must be able to manage multiple VLANs, and a single VLAN must be able to be distributed across multiple switches.

With regard to layer 2, a VLAN is logical Ethernet broadcast domain managed by one or more switches based on the use of an aggregation protocol, IEEE 802.1q.

4.3. Methods and models of IT network design

The principles and models of network design can help network engineers to design and construct a flexible, robust and manageable network.

The OSI and TCP/IP communications models should not be confused with a design model. Design models are used to build networks while complying with certain architectural rules. Their objective is to satisfy the current and future needs of businesses and their users as far as possible.

Design models facilitate the configuration, deployment, maintenance and updating of network infrastructures. They can also aid in hardware purchasing and the provision of services.

4.3.1. *Principles of structured engineering*

The adoption of a systematic design approach is highly beneficial for the implementation of a network infrastructure. It is important to remember that local area networks can be categorized according to their size:

– small network: this provides services for fewer than 200 nodes;

– medium-sized network: this serves a fleet of 200 to 1,000 nodes;

– large network: this provides services to more than 1,000 peripheral devices.

Network design varies depending on the size and needs of a company. The design of a network infrastructure for a small business with a reduced number of nodes is certainly less complex than that for a large business with a more complex infrastructure.

In general, a good design is based on the following principles of structured engineering:

– Hierarchy: the hierarchical network model is a useful tool in the design of a reliable network infrastructure. The initial complex problem is broken down into simpler elements in order to better address them. The hierarchical design model thus offers multiple distinct functional levels.

– Modularity: this stems from hierarchization. Cisco has identified several modules, including enterprise campus, service package, data center and Internet edge. Consequently, growth and change are both supported. The network is upgraded by adding new modules instead of completely rethinking the architecture of the existing network.

– Resilience: this ensures that the network infrastructure is available and operational under both normal and abnormal conditions. Normal conditions are marked by normal network flows and include planned events such as maintenance periods. Abnormal conditions are caused by software and hardware breakdowns and unplanned network flows, which occur during hardware or software breakdowns, the appearance of unanticipated traffic, intentional or unintentional DoS events or any other unanticipated event.

– Flexibility: the ability to easily modify parts of the network, add services, or improve performance without complex updates or upgrades.

– Security: this is taken into account at each level of the design model.

4.3.1.1. *Hierarchical network model*

In order to achieve these fundamental design objectives, a network infrastructure must be based on a hierarchical infrastructure. This approach enables the designer to adapt the choice of hardware and software according to the level or layer. This model is called the hierarchical model and was first introduced by Cisco.

The network will be divided into three layers. Each of these layers has a well-defined role and offers specific functions that define its role in the overall network:

– Access layer: this layer enables users to access the network. Only switches are used at this level, and sometimes hubs. Its sole purpose is to connect final users, whether by Wi-Fi, Ethernet or other means, in a secure manner if possible. Consequently, its processes are simple and its performance is not specialized. Moreover, this layer provides teleworkers and remote sites access to the company network via WAN connections.

This layer supplies several functions such as switching, port security, spanning tree protocols and power over Ethernet (PoE).

– Distribution layer: this layer links access layers and the core, enabling the routing and filtering of packets according to the strategies adopted. The network is divided into segments at this level. Routers or high-performance switches can be used at this level depending on the size of the company. For large companies, these distribution routers will ensure the aggregation of LAN or WAN links, route packets, security by applying ACLs (Access Control Lists), fault tolerance, delineate broadcast domains, etc. For small businesses using only switches, the functions mentioned above will be delegated to the core layer.

– Core layer of the network: this is also called the "backbone" of the network. This layer links the different segments of the network, specifically the floors of a business, its remote offices, etc. Routers are also found at this level; these must have extremely high performance as they are responsible for an enormous quantity of network traffic. This layer is actually made up of high-speed network devices such as the Cisco Catalyst 6500 or 6800.

Without this core layer, the switches in the distribution layer would have to be completely meshed with one another. This type of design is difficult to upgrade without taking into account the need to wire the distribution switches to one another.

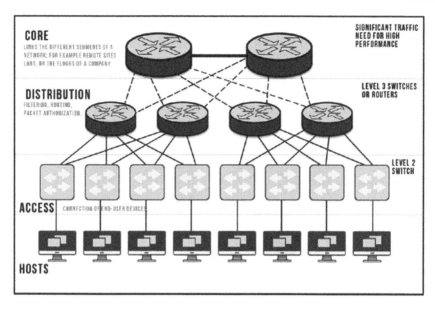

Figure 4.6. *Hierarchical model. For a color version of the figure, see www.iste.co.uk/helali/systems.zip*

Table 4.4 lists the functions of each layer of the hierarchical model.

Access layer	Distribution layer	Network core layer
Port security	High bandwidth	Very high bandwidth
Responsibility for VLANs	Gigabit/10 Gigabit	Gigabit/10 Gigabit
Power of Ethernet (PoE)	Redundancy	Redundancy
FastEthernet/GigabitEthernet	Security policy/Access control list	Link aggregation
Link aggregation		Quality of service (QoS)
Quality of service (QoS)	Link aggregation	
	Quality of service (QoS)	

Table 4.4. *Functions of layers in the hierarchical model*

Each layer has its own characteristics and needs, which influence the choice of hardware installed as well as the configurations and/or solutions implemented.

The Cisco hierarchical model is undoubtedly the most complex to implement, but it offers higher efficiency, profitability, scalability, availability and cost savings in the long term in comparison with an architecture constructed as needed and without a plan over time.

In the case of a small business, the network infrastructure is broken down into two levels: in this case, the access layer and a single layer made up of both the distribution layer and the core, called the clustered network core.

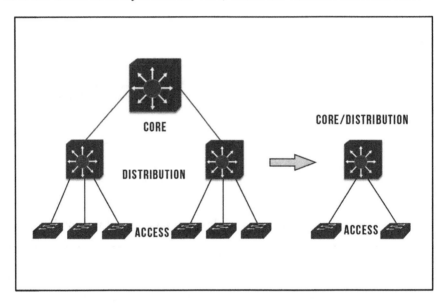

Figure 4.7. *Clustering of the distribution and core layers. For a color version of the figure, see www.iste.co.uk/helali/systems.zip*

The hierarchical network model is based on a modular design that makes it possible to upgrade the network in a simple, robust and redundant way.

This hierarchical model has numerous advantages: scalability, redundancy, performance, security, and ease of administration and maintenance.

4.3.1.2. *Design in Cisco modules*

Cisco recommends a modular network design in different "blocks", or modules in order to ensure the availability of the architecture, its ability to be easily upgraded and the management of increasingly complex network infrastructures requiring connections to dedicated data centers often located outside the main site of the business. Moreover, subsidiary sites require connectivity to the core network on the company premises and employees wishing to be able to work from home or remotely.

These modules which will be interconnected via the core network are:

– the distribution module, consisting of a group of access switches and their distribution switches. This is the most common element and the basic component of enterprise network design;

– the service module is responsible for services such as centralized LWAPP (Lightweight Access Point Protocol) controllers, unified communications services, etc.;

– the datacenter module, or server battery, is responsible for the management and updating of numerous data servers that are vital for business operations. All potential actors – employees, partners and clients of the business – rely on the datacenter's data and resources to create, collaborate and interact effectively;

– the enterprise edge module is composed of the Internet edge and the WAN edge. They are responsible for providing connectivity for vocal, video and data services internal and external to the company.

In further pursuit of the modularity of more and more sophisticated and complex network infrastructures, Cisco has also developed the Cisco Enterprise Architecture model, which breaks down the enterprise network into functional areas (also called modules) while preserving the access, distribution and network core layers.

The main components of the Cisco Enterprise Architecture model are as follows:

– Enterprise campus: this is a group of structures interconnected in the form of a scalable network, often composed of sub-modules: structural access, structural distribution, campus network core and data center. These sub-modules ensure high availability thanks to the hierarchical modular design, hardware and software redundancy, and the reconfiguration of network pathways in the event of breakdown. It also enables the optimization of network traffic and offers high-quality service and greater security.

– Enterprise edge: this provides connectivity to voice, video and data services external to the enterprise. It is at this level that security and QoS strategies can be deployed, as all the packets exchanged between the campus network and the exterior pass through this point. Intrusion detection systems (IDS) and intrusion prevention systems (IPS) can also be configured at this level.

– Service provider edge: this provides Internet services, switched telephone network services and WAN.

4.4. Assessment of needs and choice of equipment

Network infrastructure equipment must be chosen with great care. To do this, we must understand the volume and type of data transferred, all of the users involved – and their needs, to group them into VLANs, for example – as well as the servers required, and, above all, their use. Traffic-related requirements such as required output, latency and packet loss must also be taken into account.

Client and server connections must be optimized on switches to balance bandwidth. Thus, the choice of switches is an important one. There are different types of switches:

– switches with a fixed number of ports (fixed-port switches);

– modular chassis switches, to which can be added multiport cards;

– stackable switches, which are linked together by a special cable and constitute a middle ground in terms of cost between fixed-port switches and modular chassis switches.

There are other criteria that can be used in the choice of switches, such as port density (the number of ports in a switch), port output and link aggregation, which can be a solution to increase output. Another function may also be of interest, PoE, which enables IP telephones and wireless terminals to be electrically powered via Ethernet cable.

To sum up, a network must be designed hierarchically. A study of users' roles and usages should be conducted, server placement optimized and a decision made about which types of switches are to be installed: fixed, modular or stackable. Port density must also be determined, as well as output per port, link aggregation and PoE functionality for the handling of IP telephones and wireless terminals if needed.

Some design rules

– In principle, a network should be designed hierarchically. The hierarchical model is a reference point, but the network should be adapted to suit the needs of each enterprise.

– Each layer of the hierarchical model involves different configurations, particularly the access layer, which requires certain actions on the part of the administrator (status setting of each switch port, trunk installation, security, etc.).

– A study of user roles and usages should be conducted for optimized clustering.

– An optimal architecture for the network should be chosen, in particular topology design, IP ranges for different LANs/VLANs, and number of LANs/VLANs required.

– The types of switches should be carefully chosen: fixed, modular or stackable, as well as their density, output per port, link aggregation and PoE functionality.

– Each layer should contain a pair of switches.

– Each switch should be connected to the upper layer with two links for redundancy.

– Each pair of switches should be connected to the distribution layer with a link but access layer switches should not be connected to one another.

– VLANs should not be extended beyond the distribution layer.

4.5. Chapter summary

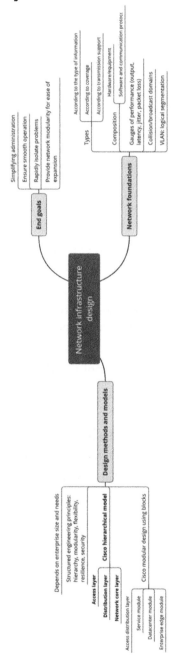

This chart is also available at www.iste.co.uk/helali/systems.zip

5

Network Services

"Think like a client."

Paul Gillin

- Defining the concept of network services.

- Understanding the different types of network services.

- Understanding the operating principle of DHCP service.

- Understanding the principle of name resolution with a DNS system.

- Understanding how the SMTP protocol functions to operate an e-mail server.

- Understanding how a web server functions.

- Understanding how a file transfer server functions.

5.1. Introduction

IT networks, which have become omnipresent in every part of human life, were designed to provide services. These services are based on the client/server approach, in which a client requests a specific service from the corresponding server.

A server is an entity that provides a service to a group of computers called clients via a network.

The services provided vary widely, ranging from file sharing, data and IT resources (printer, fax, etc.), storage, logic address attribution, e-mail, name resolution, etc.

These services depend on the needs to be met and thus differ from one enterprise to another. However, certain services are always requested, and we refer to these services as common or base services, which will be discussed throughout this chapter.

5.2. DHCP service

5.2.1. *Introduction*

DHCP (Dynamic Host Configuration Protocol) is a standardized TCP/IP protocol designed to simply manage and automate the IP address configuration. In a TCP/IP network, each computer must have a computer name and a unique IP address. The IP address (with its associated subnet mask) identifies the host computer and the sub-network to which it belongs. When a computer is moved to another sub-network, the IP address must be changed. DHCP allows an IP address to be dynamically assigned to a client, based on the database of IP addresses and managed by the local network's DHCP server.

For TCP/IP networks, DHCP reduces the complexity and amount of administrative work involved in the reconfiguration of computers. In fact, this dynamic addressing has several advantages. Only functioning stations use an address from the address space.

Modification of address parameters, that is, the default gateway address, DNS server addresses, etc., is managed by the DHCP server and provided to the computing stations.

5.2.2. *Operating principle*

The operation of the DHCP protocol is summarized in Figure 5.1.

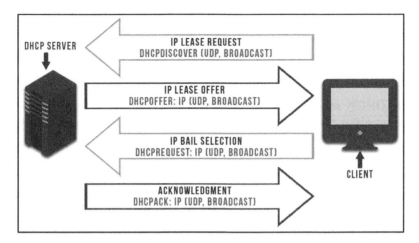

Figure 5.1. *Overall functioning of DHCP*

A device configured to use the DHCP protocol, also called the DHCP client, broadcasts upon startup an IP address request (DHCPDISCOVER) on UDP port 67 with:

– source 0.0.0.0;

– destination 255.255.255.255;

– client MAC address.

Figure 5.2. *Stage 1 of the DHCP process*

This DHCP client waits to receive an offer, which is of course issued by a DHCP server after one second. If this does not happen, it rebroadcasts its request four times, the first after 9 seconds, the second after 13 seconds, the third after 16 seconds, and the last following a random period of time between 0 and 1 second. If all four attempts fail, it repeats its request after 5 minutes.

All DHCP servers receive the request. Those configured to respond broadcast offers (DHCPOFFER) with the following information:

– client MAC address;

– an IP address;

– a subnet mask;

– a lease time (the time during which the IP address will not be used by another network device);

– its IP address.

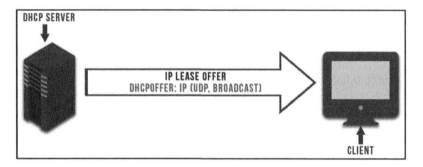

Figure 5.3. *Stage 2 of the DHCP process*

The client chooses an offer (generally the first one) and announces via broadcast that it has done so via (DHCPREQUEST). The message DHCPREQUEST includes the identification of the server selected, which now knows that its offer has been chosen, and that other DHCP servers, if they exist, must now withdraw their offers.

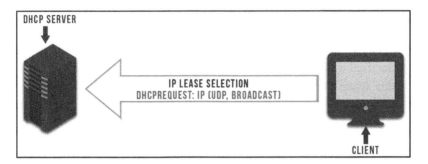

Figure 5.4. *Stage 3 of the DHCP process*

The server chosen sends an acknowledgment to the client via the message DHCPACK, which may contain other information (DNS server, gateway, etc.).

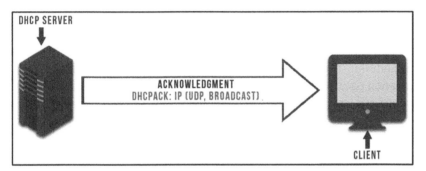

Figure 5.5. *Stage 4 of the DHCP process*

The DHCP service can be installed and configured in one of three ways:

– by installing, in Debian, for example, the isc-dhcp-server packet and modifying dhcpd.conf according to need;

– by adding the DHCP role to a Windows server;

– by configuring the DHCP service on a router.

5.2.3. *Renewal of lease*

The assignment of an IP address is temporary, as the client can use it only for a specified amount of time called the lease. Once the client obtains the lease, this lease must be renewed before its expiration via another DHCP REQUEST message. There are two ways to renew a lease:

– automatic (time triggered): if 50% of the lease period has elapsed, the client sends a DHCPREQUEST message to renew the lease. If the request is accepted, the client continues with a new lease and possibly new parameters (DHCPACK). If the server, in this case a Windows server, does not reply, the lease remains available for the remaining 50% of the initial lease time;

– manual: the user manually forces the renewal of the lease via the following commands:

- ipconfig/renew   //this command generates a DHCPREQUEST;

- ipconfig/release   //this command terminates the lease.

In addition, if a DHCP server realizes that a client lease is reaching its termination date, it can send a DHCPNAK message to ask if the client wants to extend its lease. If the server does not receive a valid reply, it releases the assigned address. In this way, the assignment of IP addresses based on leases can be optimized.

5.2.4. *The concept of a DHCP relay*

The DHCP relay agent is configured so as to relay DHCP discoveries coming from UDP port 67 toward the DHCP server. Like a DHCP server, it must have a static IP address and must recognize the IP address of the main DHCP server.

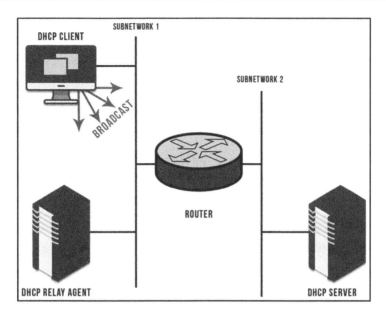

Figure 5.6. *A DHCP relay*

5.3. DNS service

5.3.1. *Introduction*

Modern networks are made up of sub-networks which are in turn composed of multiple machines accessible via their IP addresses. With the proliferation of teleinformatics networks, it has become practically impossible for users to know all the IP addresses of the machines to which they wish to connect. Consequently, these difficult-to-retain digital addresses are converted into simpler, more intuitive domain names via the DNS (Domain Name Server) service. For example, it is easier to memorize www.cisco.com than the IP address of the corresponding server, 23.50.178.229. In addition, domain names are stable, while IP addresses can change. This stability guarantees continuous access to the site in question.

5.3.2. *Operating principle*

DNS is composed of a group of servers distributed according to a hierarchized model which cooperate to automatically assign domain names to the corresponding digital IP address. This operation is referred to as *resolution*.

The name space is subdivided into zones administrated by specific servers.

Not all of the domain name correspondences of an IP address can be known by a single server. If a DNS server does not find a corresponding name, it requests information from another server, and then another, and so on until it reaches the server that knows the correspondence. There are servers responsible for a zone or with authority over this zone, for example .org, and there are resolver servers, which request the resolution of names and save the results in their cache for a certain amount of time.

Domain names are organized in tree form and read from right to left.

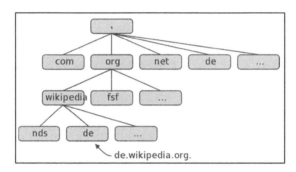

Figure 5.7. *Tree organization of domain names. For a color version of the figure, see www.iste.co.uk/helali/systems.zip*

The commands used for DNS resolution are:

- #dig www.cisco.com   for Linux systems;

- >nslookup www.cisco.com   for Windows.

The functioning of the DNS service can be summed up as follows:

– inventory and designation of domain resources via the registration of these resources;

– hierarchized organization via a naming system;

– distribution of information by zone via the recursive query mechanism;

– resolution of names in an IP address by the resolver server.

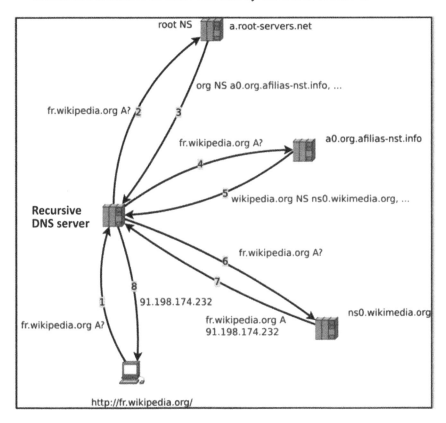

Figure 5.8. *DNS operating principle. For a color version of the figure, see www.iste.co.uk/helali/systems.zip*

Servers with authority are solely responsible for their zone and for the functioning of the DNS service. For this reason, secondary DNS servers that take over in the event of the main server breakdown should be installed. These secondary servers enable better tolerance of breakdowns.

To set up a DNS server, the BIND server can be used, or the DNS role is installed on a Windows server. It is also possible to configure a DNS server on Cisco routers, but this method is discouraged for large networks, since the DNS service requires a large amount of resources.

5.4. LDAP service

5.4.1. *Introduction*

A directory or reference that centralizes information pertaining to users and hardware and software resources facilitates and can improve the security of access to data, thus improving business performance. Use of a directory ensures consistency in the data necessary for the functioning of various applications used within the enterprise. This service is undoubtedly beneficial to any IT infrastructure as it enables better exploitation of the corresponding IT system, for which it is now the nerve center. This directory offers a solution mainly for the issues of data management, authentication and access control, which are not insignificant given their changeable and scattered nature. For reasons of interoperability, a directory should be chosen that complies with the LDAP (Lightweight Directory Access Protocol) standard in order to be able to interface with existing IT applications. The structure of the directory should reflect the internal organization of the enterprise. A directory is a system architecture component and thus ensures optimal management of users and resources.

An LDAP server is a directory service that can be queried via the LDAP protocol and whose internal structure corresponds to LDAP specifications.

The known implementations of LDAP servers are Open LDAP and Microsoft Active Directory.

The main advantages of a directory service are:

– most of the time, directories are mainly accessible for reading rather than writing;

– a directory organizes its data into a hierarchical tree form;

– sub-trees of the directory tree can be distributed over multiple hosts;

– directory tree zones can be easily administered by delegation;

– directory trees make it possible to limit a search to specified sub-trees from the start;

– numerous directory services are based on the X500 model and thus take charge of an object-oriented data model from the start.

5.4.2. *LDAP protocol*

This is a client–server protocol which defines the method the client must use to access data on the server. This protocol, which constitutes a light version of the X500 protocol or, more precisely, the DAP (Directory Access Protocol) protocol, has now been standardized by the IETF (Internet Engineering Task Force) and functions in connected mode over TCP on port 389 for LDAP and on port 636 for LDAPS (LDAP over SSL).

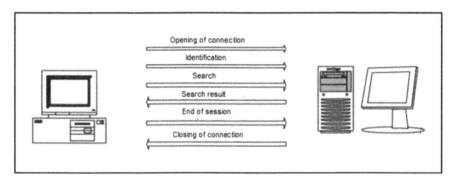

Figure 5.9. *LDAP mode of operation*

An LDAP session generally includes three stages:

– in the first stage, the LDAP client connects to the LDAP server. Other than initialization, information is also exchanged about the (extended) LDAP functionalities taken on by the client and, if necessary, authentication and negotiation concerning encryption options also take place;

– once the link has been successfully established, the client and server exchange messages with one another;

– in the final stage, the client ends the session.

The LDAP protocol provides the following functions:

– opening and closing of connection;

– search for information;

– addition, modification and deletion of information.

These functions are implemented using the procedures shown in Table 5.1.

Message	Function
bind	Start a session in which the client specifies the version of the protocol and identification information for authentication
unbind	Ends a session
search	Searches in the directory
modify	Modifies (adds, deletes, replaces) attributes of an entry
add	Adds a new entry. The client specifies the name and a list of attributes
delete	Deletes an entry
modify RDN	Modifies the RDN of an entry or of whole sub-trees
compare	Tests whether an entry corresponds to a given attribute–value pair
abandon	Tells the server that the client no longer needs the result of a specific search

Table 5.1. *List of main LDAP operations*

In addition, it enables authentication and encryption mechanisms to make information stored in the directory more secure via TLS or SSL protocols.

5.4.3. *LDAP directory*

A directory makes it possible to store data organized into categories and presented in the form of a tree, similar to a telephone directory or Yellow Pages, which contains the names of individuals, their telephone numbers and their addresses, in alphabetical order. Likewise, there are directories containing users or groups of users pertaining to different divisions of a company, directories of electronic certificates, directories of computer equipment, etc.

A directory is different from a relational database. It is designed to receive more requests in reading than in writing. It also has a tree structure and not a relational one like databases do. Additionally, a directory ensures interoperability and is also easier to replicate. Directory modifications, which are infrequent, are logged and transcribed to secondary directories.

An LDAP server stores data in tree form, called a DIT (Directory Information Tree). The structure of the DIT is determined via a standardized, expandable LDAP schema.

The root of this tree is the name of the domain that hosts the LDAP server. Entries become the branches or leaves of the tree. Each DIT entry is an LDAP object belonging to one or more categories of objects, which in their turn specify which attributes of the object are required and which are optional.

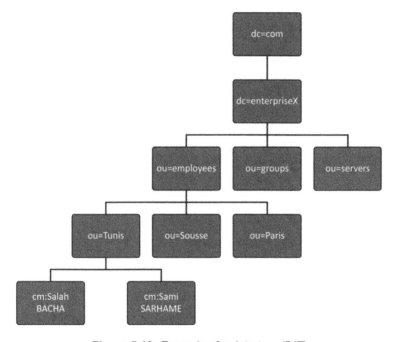

Figure 5.10. *Example of a data tree (DIT)*

Each attribute has a defined name and can contain one or more values. Attribute names include "DC" (Domain Component), "CN" (common name), "OU" (organization unit) and "SN" (surname).

Each object has an RDN (Relative Distinguished Name) unique to its level of hierarchy. The RDN composition of an object with the RDNs of its LDAP parent objects down to the root of the DIT is called the DN (Distinguished Name). Each DN is unique in the DIT and can be used to find a specified object in the object tree.

EXAMPLE.– DN: cn = Salah BACHA, or = Tunis, or: employees, dc = enterpriseX, dc:com is composed of 5 RDNs.

The objects in an LDAP directory can be queried and displayed in the form of an ASCII text using LDIF (LDAP Data Interchange Format). LDIF also defines a syntax pertaining to modifications in the directory.

The LDAP directory must be protected against various threats. The security mechanisms to be deployed have to do with:

– authentication: LDAP provides multiple levels of authentication: anonymous authentication, which allows accessible data only to be read, and key-based or certificate-based authentication with SSL;

– management of access rights by setting access rules or ACLs (Access Control Lists), which define user access rights to directory objects;

– network security: this is the definition and implementation of security mechanisms in order to make secure both access to the LDAP service and the information exchanged. SSL and TLS protocols are used to encrypt transactions.

5.5. E-mail service

5.5.1. *Introduction*

This service enables users to exchange messages via an e-mail server accessible via an IT network. To understand how an e-mail service works, we must first know a few keywords:

– MUA (Mail User Agent) is the e-mail client which acts as an interface with network services; it is an e-mail writing application such as Mozilla Thunderbird. Once the message is composed, a protocol is used to route it to the post office, initially via the MSA (Mail

Submission Agent) which acts as an intermediary between the e-mail client and the e-mail server. The protocol implemented is called SMTP;

– MTA (Mail Transfer Agent) is the e-mail transmission agent. It determines which server will take charge of the e-mail, according to the domain name contained in the e-mail address of the recipient. It is generally the e-mail server of your Internet access provider;

– MDA (Mail Delivery Agent) is considered like a mailbox where e-mails are stored while waiting for their recipient to retrieve them;

– MAA (Mail Access Agent) is the agent that enables the MUA to access an e-mail inbox.

5.5.2. *Architecture and operating principle*

The process involves eight stages (see Figure 5.11).

Stage 1: user publishes a message using his/her e-mail client (MUA).

Stage 2: message is transmitted to the sender's MTA.

Stage 3: message is transmitted to the recipient's e-mail server using the SMTP protocol (Simple Mail Transfer Protocol).

Stage 4: the server transmits the message to the MDA.

Stage 5: the MDA stores the e-mail in the recipient's e-mail inbox.

Stage 6: messages are retrieved from the e-mail inbox by the MAA with the POP (Post Office Protocol) or IMAP (Interactive Message Access Protocol) retrieval protocols.

Stage 7: messages are transmitted to the e-mail client via the POP or IMAP protocols. They are stored in the recipient's e-mail box.

Stage 8: the recipient checks his/her messages using his/her e-mail client (MUA).

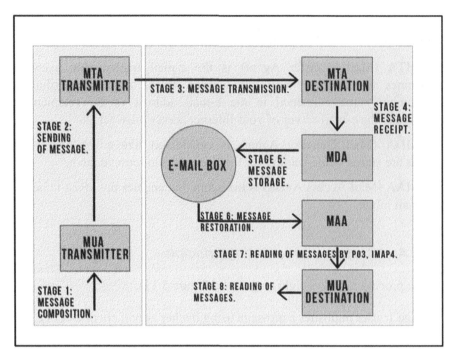

Figure 5.11. *E-mail architecture*

5.5.3. *Protocols involved*

– SMTP (Simple Mail Transfer Protocol) is responsible for transmission between an MUA and the final MTA. A receipt protocol, POP or IMAP, is used between the MDA and the final MUA.

– POP (Post Office Protocol): its main function is to process e-mails received and distribute them to their respective recipients, but it cannot send them. POP is a protocol used solely to withdraw an e-mail stored on an e-mail server. The client then copies all new messages present in its mailbox to the hard disk of its computer and can read them offline.

– IMAP (Internet Message Access Protocol) is an e-mail reading protocol. Unlike POP, it is not designed to receive and copy messages, but to read them directly from a web-based server. IMAP can manage its message directly on a remote server via authentication using a login and password.

To sum up, e-mail servers use the SMTP protocol for transmission and receipt. E-mail clients use SMTP to transmit and another protocol (POP or IMAP) for receipt.

5.6. Web server

5.6.1. *Introduction*

Web servers are used to record information and ensure that users can access it. All that is needed is a web address to retrieve an item of web content sent by a web server. HTTP or HTTPS communication protocols manage transmission between the web server and the client. They are based on IP and TCP protocols. A web server must always be connected to the Internet and hosts sites accessible by numerous different client browsers.

5.6.2. *Operating principle*

In order to display a webpage, the client uses a browser (e.g. Firefox) to send an HTTP request to the server, which decodes it and sends an HTTP response back to the browser. This is a request for specific information, such as a webpage, for example. The server searches for this information, interprets any results and sends the reply.

The most common HTTP servers are:

– Apache server: the most used web server; compatible with all operating systems;

– Microsoft Internet Information Services (IIS): for Windows systems only. Regardless of this, it is relatively complex to install;

– Nginx (created by Igor Sysoev): offers more functions than ordinary web servers. It is also higher-performing and its popularity is increasing;

– Litespeed: data transmission speed.

5.6.3. *The principle of virtual hosting*

Virtual hosting, or multi-homing, is the act of hosting multiple websites on a single server. A machine possesses a single server (virtually) hosting an infinite number of sites that have no need to be aware of one another. Generally speaking, there are two major methods of multi-homing:

– virtual hosting by address: the server machine possesses multiple IP addresses, each of which leads to a separate site. It can have one or more IP addresses or, as in this case, a single IP address, and can differentiate sites by TCP port;

– virtual hosting by name: the server machine has only a single IP address and site names direct the request;

– a combination of the two methods (by both IP address and name) is also possible.

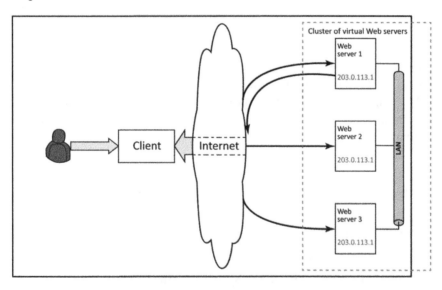

Figure 5.12. *Virtual web servers*

5.6.3.1. *Virtual hosting by network address (IP/TCP port)*

Network hosting consists of having available multiple TCP ports and/or multiple IP addresses (physical or virtual) on the server machine.

The Linux command *ifconfig* is used to configure network interfaces. For multiple addresses, it must be specified to Apache, for example, which ones should be listened on, and on which TCP ports, using the directive *Listen.*

```
Example of virtual Apache hosts based on the network:IP/ports

Listen 80
Listen 192.168.0.2:81

<VirtualHost 192.168.0.1:80>
DocumentRoot /var/www1
ServerName server1
</Virtualhost>

<VirtualHost 192.168.0.2:80>
DocumentRoot /var/www2
ServerName server2
</VirtualHost>

<VirtualHost 192.168.0.2:81>
DocumentRoot /var/www3
ServerName server3
</VirtualHost>
```

Figure 5.13. *Virtual hosting by IP address and ports (Apache)*

5.6.3.2. *Virtual hosting by names*

We have a single IP address and a single port: 192.168.0.1:80. The DNS server has been configured to link this IP address to two different domain names, server1 and server2.

```
Listen 192.168.0.1:80

ServerName DefaultServer
DocumentRoot /var/www

NameVirtualHost 192.168.0.1:80

<VirtualHost 192.168.0.1:80>
ServerName server1
DocumentRoot /var/www1
</VirtualHost>

<VirtualHost 192.168.0.1:80>
ServerName server2
DocumentRoot /var/www2
</VirtualHost>
```

Figure 5.14. *Virtual hosting by names*

5.6.3.3. *Virtual hosting by name and by IP*

Take a server listening to 192.168.0.1:80 and 192.168.0.2:80. It must serve the names server1, server2, server3 and server4. Playing with NameVirtualHost, we will tell Apache the first direction, that of the IP/port. Once this direction has been carried out, Apache will analyze the name in the *Host* header and direct it into the <VirtualHost> block, which specifies it with the directive ServerName.

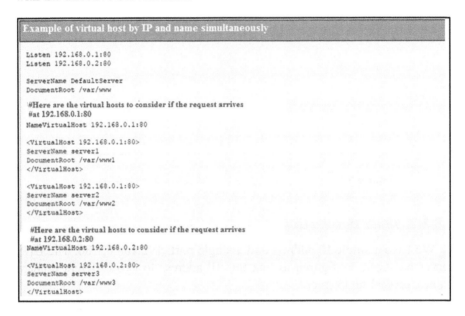

Figure 5.15. *Virtual host by IP and name*

5.7. FTP file transfer service

5.7.1. *Definition*

FTP (File Transfer Protocol) is a file transfer protocol. This transfer is executed via a connection between an FTP server and a client located on a computer. Online posting, increase in the number of documents online and website maintenance are frequently carried out via this protocol. The secure variant is FTPS.

5.7.2. *Operating principle*

The FTP protocol is based on the TCP protocol. To access an FTP server, an FTP client is required. This client can function via command line (ftp, Curl) or in graphic mode (Filezilla).

It provides two types of connection:

– control connection: for the transmission of commands from the client to the server. These commands have to do with file transfer, renaming, deletion, etc.;

– data connection: for pure data transmission. It can be launched from the client or the server.

There are several FTP servers, including but not limited to:

– ProFTPd;

– PureFTPd;

– VsFTPd.

5.7.3. *Types*

There are two types of FTP servers:

– protected FTP: a password must be supplied to access it (business, university course, UVT, etc.);

– anonymous FTP, for which access is direct and transparent, or can be gained by filling out a form with "anonymous" or sometimes "FTP" as the login name and "your e-mail address" (or other terms) as the password.

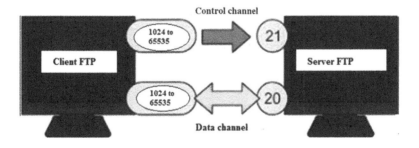

Figure 5.16. *FTP architecture*

5.8. Chapter summary

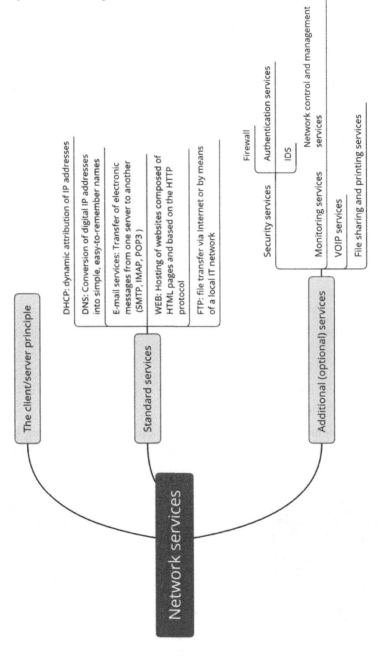

This chart is also available at www.iste.co.uk/helali/systems.zip

6

System and Network Security

"A computer is only secure when it's turned off, and not really even then!"

Bill Gates

– Recalling the basic concepts and challenges of IT security.

– Defining the threats and attacks to which a business's IT system can be exposed.

– Describing various security mechanisms.

– Understanding security management systems and corresponding norms as well as the concept of a security policy.

6.1. Introduction

These days, business IT systems are more and more widely distributed and rely on computer networks to connect the headquarters with its various subsidiaries, as well as teleworkers, retail establishments, etc. This remote access has encouraged the decentralization of businesses and their opening up to the entire world, and has become increasingly sophisticated with new wireless access technologies (GSM, 4/5G, Wimax) and the complete opening up of the Internet network.

Of course, IT networks are necessary for businesses as they enable trade and increase these businesses' competitiveness. Nevertheless, they also carry enormous risks such as the interception of messages, data theft, loss of system and network access, hacking, etc. A wide range of security and safeguarding mechanisms have been introduced in order to reduce the risks faced by businesses as much as possible.

6.2. Definitions, challenges and basic concepts

IT security is made up of all of the technical, organizational, legal and human procedures deployed to maintain and ensure the security of the hardware and software resources of an enterprise's IT system.

Security represents a major challenge for any business and its partners. There are in fact multiple challenges to a company's competitiveness and even survival in an atmosphere of increasingly sophisticated attacks and threats:

– short-term challenges: giving all authorized users access to the information they need;

– intermediate-term challenges: these have to do with the consistency of the enterprise's information system;

– long-term challenges: keeping users' and clients' trust for a good business brand image.

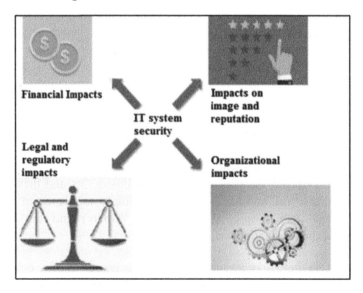

Figure 6.1. *Various impacts of security*

Information is as important an asset as those related to the classic production system (physical assets, human assets, financial assets, etc.). It is even a strategic asset that must be protected. Information security can be defined as a system implemented to ensure the protection of this information and its related assets with the goal of mainly ensuring the following services or objectives:

– availability: ensuring that authorized users have access to information and related resources when desired;

– integrity: ensuring precision and accuracy of information during storage, processing and transmission;

– confidentiality: ensuring that only authorized persons can access information.

In addition to the concept of CIA (Confidentiality, Integrity and Availability), other principles or services may be necessary for the protection of information, such as:

– authenticity: the fact of an entity actually being what it claims to be;

– nonrepudiation: the fact of not being able to deny a transaction that has been made. It consists of obtaining proof of the transmission of information, or of its receipt;

– traceability: this is the characteristic that preserves traces of the condition and movements of information. It involves retracing histories and the use or localization of information by means of a documenting mechanism.

Security can be broken down to encompass multiple levels:

– prevention: protects a business's assets from being attacked;

– detection: determining when, how and by whom an asset has been damaged;

– reaction: being able, after a security-related incident, to restore assets or reduce the impact of the incident.

IT system security encompasses physical security against theft and incidents of force majeure (fire, earthquake, floods), software security (operating systems and applications), human security (employee awareness) and organizational security.

IT system security generally involves measures against threats, vulnerabilities and attacks:

– threats: events likely to occur that would be harmful to the business's resources;

– vulnerabilities: characteristics inherent to an asset that may constitute a weakness or flaw related to IT security. These vulnerabilities can be organizational (no security policy), human (staff not trained), software-related (design and programming errors) or hardware-related (use of unreliable products);

– attacks: malicious actions that harm the security of an asset. An attack represents the concretization of a threat and/or requires the exploitation of a vulnerability.

6.3. Threats/attacks

Attacks include any action that may compromise the security and functioning of an IT system. There are multiple motivations for attacks including the theft of sensitive information, disruption of system operation, use of system resources for other purposes, etc.

The process of an attack begins with the collection of information pertaining to the system targeted, and then the determination of corresponding vulnerabilities, followed by the execution of the attack proper and finally removal of the traces of this attack.

Attacks can be grouped into four categories.

6.3.1. Access attacks

Any attempt to access information by an unauthorized person. This type of attack affects confidentiality of information. Sniffing, social engineering and password hacking are examples of this type of attack.

6.3.2. *Modification attacks*

Any attempt to modify information. This type of attack targets information integrity. Viruses, worms and Trojan horses are examples of this type of attack.

6.3.3. *Saturation attacks*

The intent of this type of attack is to overwhelm a company's server and paralyze its website for several hours, thus blocking access to it without necessarily altering its content. These attacks target the availability of information. TCP SYN flood attacks, smurfing, ping flood attacks and UDP flood attacks are some examples of this type of attack.

6.3.4. *Repudiation attacks*

These attacks target responsibility. In other words, repudiation consists of denying that an event or transaction has actually taken place. Frauds such as MAC spoofing, IP spoofing and man-in-the-middle are examples of repudiation attacks.

6.4. Security mechanisms

Security mechanisms are means deployed to detect, prevent and fight against a security attack on the assets of an IT system.

An IT system with its professional and system assets needs security mechanisms to ensure basic levels of security, that is, availability, integrity and confidentiality, and, if possible, the remaining levels of security, authenticity and nonrepudiation, as well.

There are various defensive resources available. We generally do not limit ourselves to a single means of securitization, but rather tend to favor a deep defense approach which consists of installing multiple security technologies in order to reduce the risk that any one security component will be compromised or break down.

The concept of deep defense is based on the superimposition of multiple levels of defense in order to have layers of security ready to act if the business's primary security mechanism has been attacked.

6.4.1. *Encryption tools*

These days, the goal of encryption is to address issues of communications security in general and to provide a number of security services such as confidentiality, authentication, integrity, etc.

Encryption algorithms, hash functions, electronic signatures and digital certificates are some of the best-known examples of these tools.

6.4.2. *Antivirus programs*

These programs detect and eliminate viruses, worms and Trojan horses, as well as other malware that can infect computers.

6.4.3. *Firewalls/IDS and IPS*

6.4.3.1. *Firewalls*

Hardware or software firewalls are used to isolate areas of a network and to authorize only certain flows in by filtering packets exchanged, in order to prevent intrusions.

This filtering of packets takes place in the TCP/IP layer. Incoming and outgoing packets are examined in terms of their source and destination IP addresses and their port numbers in order to be authorized to pass or not. Packet filtering functions with positive filtering rules, that is, what should be authorized must be defined, and anything not explicitly authorized is automatically forbidden.

This static packet filtering is enriched by additional rules to create what is called *Stateful Packet Inspection* (SPI). SPI verifies that incoming data packets are related to data packets previously sent, that is, that they belong to a session initiated by the secured local network.

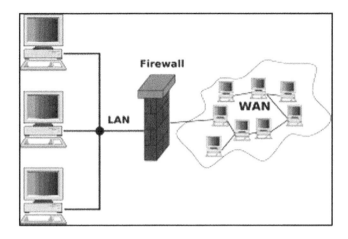

Figure 6.2. *The role of a firewall*

Most businesses have web and e-mail servers they wish to make accessible to external visitors. These servers are thus placed between the private network and the Internet on a separate segment of the network. This segment is governed by less rigid security rules and is thus accessible from the outside, but relatively isolated from the local network. Its objective is to prevent exterior access to private machines in the business's internal network. This isolated network segment is called a demilitarized zone (DMZ).

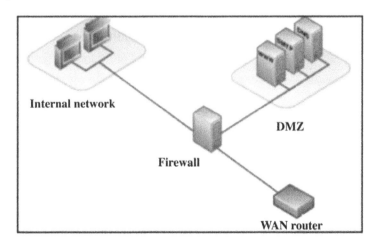

Figure 6.3. *Demilitarized zone (DMZ)*

Proxies are a specific type of firewall consisting of an intermediary or proxy server that relays requests from the internal network to an external network, generally the Internet. These proxies also offer other functionalities such as caching, authentication, anonymization and more refined filtering using advanced filters.

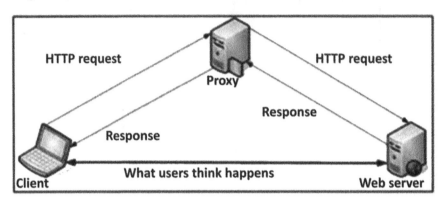

Figure 6.4. *Proxy operating principle*

6.4.3.2. *Intrusion detection systems (IDS) and intrusion prevention systems (IPS)*

IDSs/IPSs detect and warn of malicious behaviors by monitoring processes, for example, or observing certain aspects of user and program behavior to detect suspicious activity based on pre-established rules or statistics. Honeypots are practical tools to detect intrusions.

6.4.4. *VPNs*

These are virtual private networks constructed over a public network (the Internet). They provide secure, cost-efficient WAN links using encryption and tunneling techniques and are being used with increasing frequency by businesses. A tunnel is a logical connection between arbitrary end points which are VPN clients, servers or gateways.

There are two methods of creating tunnels. In the first one, the tunnel is established in layer 3 of the OSI layer model. Another method directly involves layer 2 of the OSI layer model, with the data packet from layer 3 being encrypted and then addressed with the physical address.

There are also site-to-site VPNs and remote access VPNs. The main protocols are PPTP, L2TP, IPSEC and MPLS. The choice depends on the performance and security requirements of the business in question:

– PPTP (Point-to-point Tunneling Protocol): a data link layer protocol responsible for data encryption and compression. It is included in Windows operating systems since it was developed by Microsoft. Its use is especially recommended for remote access.

– L2TP (Layer 2 Tunneling Protocol): a more advanced version of PPTP and L2F. The structure and advantages of these two non-standardized methods have been adopted and standardized into L2TP. While PPTP supports only the IP, IPX and NetBEUI protocols, the L2TP protocol has the advantage of being able to transport any network protocol into the PPP frame structure. This means that it also has a significant overload and thus a low net data output. The L2TP protocol works well with point-to-point virtual private networks as well as remote access connections to service providers.

– IPSEC: a protocol that secures data exchange in the network layer. It is an extension of the Internet protocol (IP) that includes encryption and authentication mechanisms. This makes it possible to transport secured IP packets cryptographically over public, unsecured networks. It is based on two mechanisms. The first mechanism, AH (Authentication Header), is designed to ensure the integrity and authenticity of IP datagrams. The data transmitted is not encrypted, so this mode does not guarantee confidentiality of exchanges. The second mechanism, ESP (Encapsulating Security Payload), ensures authentication as well as confidentiality via data encryption. Both mechanisms are based on the IKE (Internet Key Exchange) protocol, which manages the keys used.

IPSec has two operating modes: transport and tunnel.

Transport mode is relatively easy to set up but has the disadvantage of not masking the IP address since the external header is produced by the IP layer. This mode is usually used between two hosts. In tunnel mode, data passes through the battery of protocols until it reaches the IP layer, and then the IPSec layer adds a new header to it, thus ensuring address masking. Tunnel mode is recommended for use between two security gateways (router, firewall, etc.) in order to link two remote sites, for example.

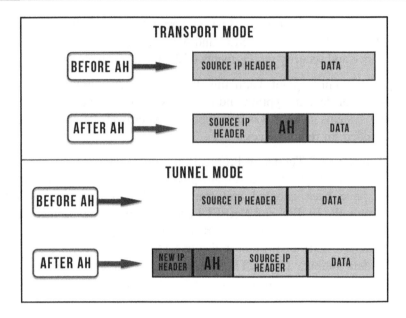

Figure 6.5. *IPsec operating modes with AH mechanism. For a color version of the figure, see www.iste.co.uk/helali/systems.zip*

– MPLS (Multi-Protocol Label Switching) combines the advantages of switching with routing. It operates between layers 2 and 3 of the OSI layer model and is based on label switching. VPN creation is one of its multiple functions. Practically speaking, to create client VPNS, each client flow must be isolated. To do this, the MPLS label is now composed not of one label but of two; the first (exterior) label identifies the path toward the destination LSR (Label Switch Router) and changes with each hop, while the second (interior) label specifies the VPN-ID assigned to the VPN and is not modified between the source LSR and the destination LSR.

The components of MPLS VPNs are as follows:

– the CE router (Customer Edge router) represents the client router connected to the IP backbone via an access service (LS, Frame Relay, ATM, etc.);

– the PE router (Provider Edge router) is the backbone router to which CEs are connected. It enables a CE to belong to a given VPN. The role of the PE consists of managing VPNs by cooperating with other PEs and switching frames with P routers;

– the P router (Provider router) is responsible for MPLS frame switching.

The operator manages the VPNs in the backbone via PEs. Each PE assigns a VRF (Virtual Routing and Forwarding Table) to each of its user interfaces. The VRF is a routing table assigned to a VPN which gives the paths toward the IP networks corresponding to this VPN.

6.4.5. *Other means of security*

6.4.5.1. *VLANs*

These make it possible to structure networks into zones sealed by activity, thus improving the security of the overall network infrastructure. VLANs represent an example of logical segmentation technology used to divide up the broadcast domain and to ensure that each VLAN can communicate with another VLAN only after routing configuration and installation of ACLs corresponding to the company's security policy.

6.4.5.2. *Means of authentication*

This can be done via login and password or by a chip card or biometry. In the first case, a strict policy of the choice and management of passwords must be implemented. Authentication can also be carried out via electronic certificates. In this case, the IEEE802.1X protocol can be jointly deployed with a Radius-type server.

6.4.5.3. *Logical access control*

This specifies the actions a previously authenticated user is authorized to take with the IT system's various resources. It depends, naturally, on the physical access control. There are several models of logical access control available, including MAC (Mandatory Access Control), DAC (Discretionary Access Control) and RBAC (Role-Based Access Control).

6.4.5.4. *Physical security of equipment and premises*

This consists of providing for the deployment of barriers, alarm systems, surveillance cameras, locks and other physical mechanisms to manage physical access to a business's premises, servers, computers and network equipment.

6.4.5.5. *NAT (Network Address Translation)*

This is a mechanism that makes it possible to replace the private IP addresses of machines in the local network with public addresses during traversal of an NAT router. The main objective of this technology is to compensate for the shortage of IPv4 addresses. Moreover, it enables internal local network IP addresses to be masked, thus improving security.

6.4.5.6. *NAC (Network Access Control)*

NACis a protective concept that provides:

– clear recognition of attempts to access and identify devices and users;

– verification that security policies adopted are in place;

– isolation and, as far as possible, automatic correction of violations of established policy;

– creation and management of policies and assessment of incidents and data collected.

6.4.5.7. *Logging and audit*

Logging allows traces of various activities to be retained; more precisely, who did what, when and for how long for each incoming and outgoing connection. Logging makes security more dynamic as it is regularly reviewed in order to monitor developments in systems, networks and risks.

6.4.5.8. *Backups*

Backups keep an intact, functional copy of an information system's data and documentation, allowing activity to be resumed in the event of an incident. Data storage technologies such as Storage Area Networks (SANs) or Network Attached Storage (NAS) are more suitable for a modern information system. Backup and restoration procedures and devices should be chosen according to need, strictly implemented and regularly verified.

6.4.5.9. *Training and awareness*

Information system security involves a human and social component that is as important as the technological component. Even the best protection methods will fail if they are in the hands of inexperienced, untrained, ill-informed users. Therefore, the managers of technical infrastructures and networks must work to inform, train and increase awareness among users with regard to security issues. They must also stay informed about new attacks and threats, subscribe to alert bulletins from CERT and other organizations that broadcast information on security and to specialized journals, consult specialized forums regularly, attend conferences on the subject and, above all, apply the lessons learned.

Security service	Means of security
Confidentiality	Encryption techniques
Integrity	Hash functions
Availability	Redundancy, backup
Authenticity	Certificate, biometry
Nonrepudiation	Signature, electronic notary

Table 6.1. *Security means and services*

6.5. Security management systems: norms and security policies

6.5.1. *Norms*

Security is multidisciplinary. It has multiple aspects, in this context ethical, legislative, technological, methodological and normative.

The securitization of an information system is a relatively arduous task requiring an IT security management system to guide it.

A management system is defined by the ISO as "a system enabling the establishment of a policy and objectives and the attainment of these objectives". It can be considered as a set of organizational measures and techniques targeting specific objectives. These systems are based on reference sources that formalize policies and procedures so that they can be subsequently audited.

The implementation of these information security management systems, or ISMS, requires material, human and financial resources, an investment that is justifiable insofar as these security management systems increase reliability. Moreover, the fact of being audited or even certified by a standardization organization increases trust and confidence in a business on the part of its partners.

The 2700X family of ISO norms sets the standards for information security management systems (ISMS). We are referring more specifically here to norm ISO27001, which sets requirements for the setup of an ISMS, and norm ISO27002, which provides a catalogue of best practices for information security management.

Norm ISO27001 relies on a process-based approach, and more precisely on the Deming wheel process, or PDCA model (for Plan, Do, Check, Act):

– the Plan phase consists of defining the perimeter to be secured, gauging the risks and selecting security measures;

– the Do phase consists of planning how risks will be addressed, designing significant indicators, training personnel and managing incidents;

– the Check phase uses controls, audits and review to regularly assess the current state of the information system's security;

– the Act phase involves the implementation of corrective, preventive and improvement-related actions in the event that the predetermined objectives have not been met.

6.5.2. *The idea of security policy*

The ITSEC (Information Technology Security Evaluation Criteria) European standard defines a security policy as being "the laws, rules, and practices that govern the way in which sensitive information and other resources are managed, protected, and distributed within a specific system".

It is concretized by a set of reference documents which include the security rules to be applied and complied with. It also defines the security objectives set by the business and the mechanisms and procedures deployed to ensure them.

The securitization of an organization or enterprise's network and system infrastructures must be based on the security policy in effect. The choice and implementation of different security mechanisms and solutions depends on the corresponding security policy.

6.6. Chapter summary

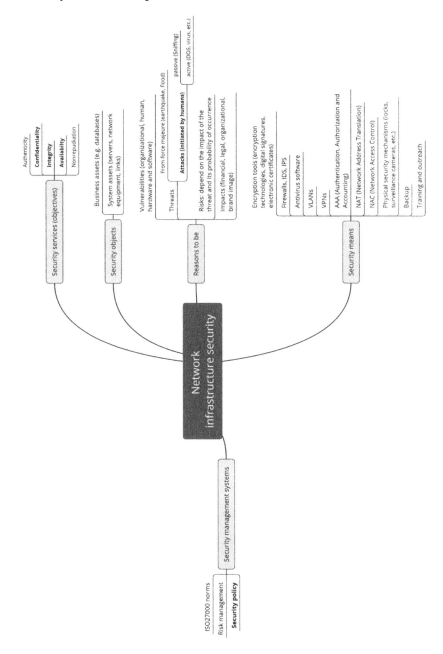

This chart is also available at www.iste.co.uk/helali/systems.zip

7

Virtualization and Cloud Computing

"You don't need to be physically out in the world anymore to participate in it. I'm 90% virtual."

Karl Lagerfeld

– Understanding the concept of virtualization

– Learning the virtualization domains

– Determining the advantages and disadvantages of virtualization

– Understanding the different types of virtualization

– Understanding the concept of cloud computing

– Learning the different service models pertaining to cloud computing and their typologies

7.1. Introduction

The setting up or upgrading of IT infrastructures requires significant financial investment for every business. In an increasingly difficult economic climate, any solution that enables a reduction in costs is more than relevant. This category includes virtualization, which helps businesses to create an IT infrastructure that is easy to manage and low cost, thus eliminating dependence on a single hardware provider and ensuring more resilient, flexible and agile IT functions.

Additionally, cloud computing, based on the concept of virtualization, is of great interest to businesses insofar as it enables a new way of organizing information systems as well as another approach to managing different IT resources. The goal remains higher profitability for the business, as well as scalability and the capacity for expansion.

7.2. Virtualization

7.2.1. *Definition*

Virtualization includes a range of technologies offering IT resources that can be used flexibly and on demand, independently of the underlying hardware infrastructure. It can be seen as a layer that separates the operating system from the hardware so that the various resources can operate more efficiently. This layer helps to create an environment suited to specifications instead of adapting specifications to fit within the limitations of the hardware environment.

A piece of IT hardware is initially designed to make a single operating system and several applications function. Virtualization makes it possible to bypass this limitation and run multiple operating systems on the same hardware support, thus optimizing the use of hardware resources.

Virtualization can affect the entirety of the hardware environment, that is, the processor, memory, hard disk, peripheral devices and network components, so that each virtual machine has its own virtual resources. Consequently, every virtual machine is completely independent and will not be disturbed or disrupted by the functioning of other virtual machines (shutdown, startup, installation of programs, etc.) that may coexist on the same physical machine.

7.2.2. *Benefits of virtualization*

Virtualization technology offers a number of benefits:

– pooling of resources: the setting up of multiple logically separated systems on a single physical machine optimizes the use of these systems;

– ease of configuration, deployment, upgrading and migration of virtual machines;

– ability to test a new system without disrupting the base operating system;

– reduction of operating energy consumption: using less hardware results in lower electricity consumption and fewer upkeep and maintenance operations;

– improved security: network security is increased because guest operating systems are not visible to attackers;

– improved availability: a cluster can be formed of two physical servers with virtual machines, which can be automatically copied from one server to another in the event of problems. Moreover, the snapshot or instant capture function of a virtual server makes it possible easily to reinstall a server configuration;

– improved prevention and management of malfunctions as well as system activity resumption thanks to automatic recovery. Virtual servers can be simply restored in the event of problems due to their portability, since the physical server sees them as a series of files;

– scalability via the rapid deployment of new application servers;

– the supervision function is greatly simplified and centralized; a single monitoring software program supervises all virtual servers.

7.2.3. *Areas of application*

7.2.3.1. *Virtualization of applications*

The virtualization of applications consists of adding an additional software layer between an application and the operating system through which all file reading, modification or system registry files must pass in order to redirect them transparently toward a virtual location. The end goal is to improve portability and compatibility of applications by isolating them from the host operating system. In this way, multiple applications can function on a single operating system without encountering compatibility problems, in the registry, for example. It is also possible for multiple versions of one application to run on a single operating system. Wine, PlayOnLinux and CrossOver are some examples of this.

7.2.3.2. Virtualization of servers

The principle here is to make multiple virtual servers function on a single physical server in order to optimize the use of its capacity. Studies have shown that servers use an average of 15% of their capacity. This technique enables a business to save in terms of physical infrastructures, specifically with regard to space occupied, electricity consumption, climate control and staff needed for administration.

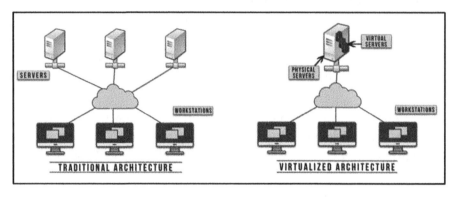

Figure 7.1. *Virtualization of servers. For a color version of the figure, see www.iste.co.uk/helali/systems.zip*

7.2.3.3. Virtualization of storage

The objective of this is to provide advanced functionality in terms of storage. The principle is that various storage resources are brought together into a single logical storage device. This procedure, also called storage abstraction, enables the user (server, application or workstation) to access only one logical storage resource through an intermediary layer composed of servers, software and network switches, which intercepts outgoing server traffic and transfers it to physical storage devices according to specific protocols.

This virtualization ensures independence between the management of the physical storage system (disks, storage bays) and its attached servers, and enables applications to separate the physical management of disks (and storage bays) from the servers that use them, which also reduces the high cost of storage management.

Storage virtualization enables:

– the addition of a new storage device without interruption of service;

– the conglomeration of multiple heterogeneous storage devices into a single logical storage entity;

– dynamic reallocation of storage space according to application server needs.

This virtualization is used in NAS and SAN networks.

7.2.3.4. *Virtualization of networks*

The virtualization of networks is based on the abstraction of hardware network resources in software form. It separates network services from the hardware on which they operate. Physical network resources, specifically switches and routers, are thus accessible via the intermediary of a centralized management system. This procedure increases the network's productivity and efficiency.

More specifically, it involves transforming certain network functionalities (firewall, NAT, etc.) into software programs. In this way, the deployment or updating of new network functionalities is greatly simplified and less costly as well.

The management of these virtualized network functions is carried out by a network controller called an SDN (Software-Defined Network) controller, which controls the network, improves its performance and automates its services.

7.2.3.5. *Virtualization of workstations*

Workstation functionality is supplied based on a virtual infrastructure. This approach is beneficial because it ensures centralized, simplified administration of IT facilities as well as the substitution for traditional workstations with clients that are both more cost-effective and more eco-friendly.

In addition, it fulfills the need for continuous access from anywhere, a mobility requirement that is increasingly omnipresent for businesses today. Thus, traditional desktops, which are cumbersome and become obsolete within 2–3 years, are replaced by virtual desktops, or VDI (Virtual Desktop Integration).

This form of virtualization also relieves businesses of the need to manage their own IT facilities and the associated maintenance burden. Each user can access his or her own work environment hosted on virtual servers in datacenters.

7.2.4. *Categories of virtualization*

Virtualization, a way to supply a number of IT resources independent of the hardware platform, can be broken down into four categories according to Figure 7.2.

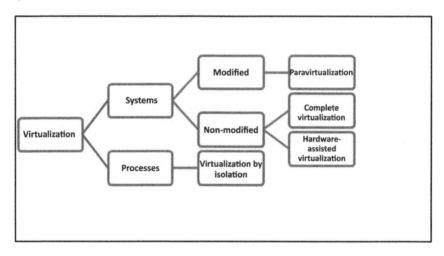

Figure 7.2. *Categories of virtualization*

7.2.4.1. *Virtualization by isolation*

This category can pertain to applications or processes and is based on confining the execution of applications to well-defined contexts using a specific software program, making it possible to run several instances of the same application. Open VZ provides an example of process virtualization.

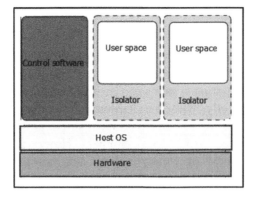

Figure 7.3. *Virtualization by isolation. For a color version of the figure, see www.iste.co.uk/helali/systems.zip*

7.2.4.2. *Paravirtualization or type 1 hypervisor*

A hypervisor functions directly on hardware, thus avoiding using a complete host operating system and limiting itself to the basic kernel services of common operating systems, in this case the management of virtual machine memory and scheduling. In this situation, the guest operating system is modified and acknowledges that it has been virtualized and then relies on the hypervisor to access the hardware resources of the physical server. This category of virtualization shows high performance but is costly. Examples include VMsphere(ESXi), KVM and Microsoft Hyper V.

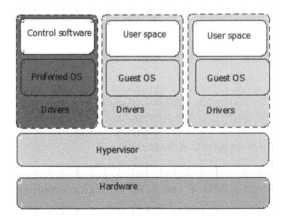

Figure 7.4. *Paravirtualization. For a color version of the figure, see www.iste.co.uk/helali/systems.zip*

7.2.4.3. *Complete virtualization*

This type of virtualization is also called a type 2 hypervisor. It is based on an emulator running on a classic operating system used to manage the memory and scheduling of virtual machines. The hardware is completely simulated. Other operating systems can be installed; these will think they are communicating directly with the hardware. This type of virtualization enables multiple systems to cohabitate on a single physical machine while remaining partitioned from one another. However, it is not very high-performing. Guest operating systems are not aware that they are virtualized. Examples of this approach include VirtualBox, Oracle VM and HyperV.

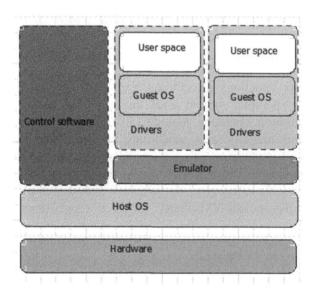

Figure 7.5. *Complete virtualization. For a color version of the figure, see www.iste.co.uk/helali/systems.zip*

7.2.4.4. *Hardware-assisted virtualization*

This represents an improvement on complete virtualization using the processor extensions AMD-V and Intel VT. The simplicity of function of applications and the available of high-performance administrative tools have contributed greatly to the success of this type of virtualization. Examples of this category include VMWare, VirtualBox and Virtual PC.

7.2.5. *Limits of virtualization*

Despite the significant benefits of virtualization technology, there are some disadvantages.

The physical machine or server hosting various virtual machines must be extremely powerful and equipped with state-of-the-art technologies. It must possess several processors, consistent memory and high storage capacity. These characteristics are, of course, very costly.

The major issue with virtualization is the possibility of the physical server encountering problems or breaking down. If this happens, the virtual machines become unavailable.

Performance may be reduced by the use of virtualization, which can hinder applications from running, as virtualization itself takes up around 30% of the machine load. However, this drop in performance will have more or less of an effect depending on the type of virtualization adopted.

A security breach in the hypervisor exposes all virtual machines to security risks. Virtual systems become preferred targets for attackers, especially if they are not regularly updated and patched.

7.3. Cloud computing

7.3.1. *Definitions*

Wikipedia defines cloud computing as a concept that consists of siting IT processes on remote servers that are traditionally executed on local servers or at a user workstation.

NIST (National Institute for Standards and Technology) defines cloud computing as access via a telecommunications network, on demand and by self-service, to shared, virtualized IT resources. It is a relocation of a business's IT infrastructure.

Cloud computing represents an economic IT model that enables the use of software and hardware resources involving servers that are not owned by a company via the Internet, generally by payment-on-demand and according to the company's needs. The goal is to share IT resources including computational power, storage space and network functionalities.

7.3.2. *Leverage factors and generic principles*

Several factors have contributed greatly to the emergence and success of the cloud computing paradigm.

Successive developments in IT systems, such as the increasing of computational power with new processors, the meteorically swift development of Web technologies, the opening up of companies to the Internet and the current trend toward decentralization have led logically to cloud computing. The current environment, which is highly competitive and based on cost reduction, the appearance of new, increasingly sophisticated terminals, etc., provides an ideal context for cloud computing.

Cloud computing represents a method of organizing and relocating the components that make up an IT system. It is based mainly on the concept of virtualization. The end user is able to execute applications according to his or her own needs without knowing where the servers or the data used are located.

Cloud computing is characterized by the following features:

– continuous and up-to-date availability of services;

– bespoke operation, with payment made according to consumption;

– dynamic allocation of capacity according to load for better management of traffic peaks and sharing of resources.

7.3.3. *Architecture models*

Cloud computing is generally broken down into three main service models that differ according to the degree of outsourcing adopted by the company's IT system. These three models illustrate three levels of virtualization and can also be considered delivery models.

The objective of the cloud concept is to set up a service between a client and a service provider while ensuring the continuity and quality of this service. To achieve this goal, methods in all levels involved have been developed, including:

– the application, used by the client;

– the platform, or the environment that executes the application;

– the infrastructure, which constitutes the platform support.

7.3.3.1. IaaS (Infrastructure as a Service)

Hosting concerns a virtual infrastructure made up of servers, network resources, storage solutions, etc. It is the equivalent of a real infrastructure and is made available by the cloud provider. The client purchases its resources according to need. Thus, the whole infrastructure part of the client company is outsourced. This model is the base for the following two models, Amazon EC2 and Google Cloud Storage, which are examples of this model.

7.3.3.2. PaaS (Platform as a Service)

The cloud provider offers the whole development platform, hosting company applications as well as management and testing environments accessible through a browser with no need to use other software programs. The degree of outsourcing is higher than that of the IaaS model. This model is more relevant to applications developers, as it provides them with a customized development framework. It also serves as a base for the SaaS model. An example of a PaaS is Google App Engine.

7.3.3.3. SaaS (Software as a Service)

Business applications are transferred to the cloud provider, meaning that all necessary software programs are functional without any prior installation or updating, and require no maintenance on the part of the client. This model supplies the highest degree of outsourcing and is based mainly on the principle of standardization of hosted applications. SaaS platforms are based on SOA (Service Oriented Architecture); examples include Gmail and Office 365.

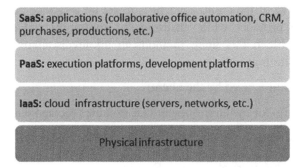

Figure 7.6. *Cloud service models*

The cloud is a solution that provides space for virtual placement of server or network infrastructures, development or execution platforms, applications, etc. A cloud supports different layers of the service model, from infrastructure to the end client.

INTERNAL MODEL	IAAS MODEL	PAAS MODEL	SAAS MODEL
APPLICATION CODE	APPLICATION CODE	APPLICATION CODE	APPLICATION CODE
DATA	DATA	DATA	DATA
CORE SOFTWARE	CORE SOFTWARE	CORE SOFTWARE	CORE SOFTWARE
OPERATING SYSTEMS	OPERATING SYSTEMS	OPERATING SYSTEMS	OPERATING SYSTEMS
VIRTUALIZATION LAYERS	VIRTUALIZATION LAYERS	VIRTUALIZATION LAYERS	VIRTUALIZATION LAYERS
HARDWARE PLATFORMS	HARDWARE PLATFORMS	HARDWARE PLATFORMS	HARDWARE PLATFORMS
STORAGE NETWORK	STORAGE NETWORK	STORAGE NETWORK	STORAGE NETWORK
BACKUP NETWORK	BACKUP NETWORK	BACKUP NETWORK	BACKUP NETWORK
INTERNAL NETWORK	PRIVATE NETWORK	PRIVATE NETWORK	PRIVATE NETWORK
EXTERNAL NETWORK	EXTERNAL NETWORK	EXTERNAL NETWORK	EXTERNAL NETWORK
EXTERNALPARTNERS	EXTERNALPARTNERS	EXTERNALPARTNERS	EXTERNALPARTNERS
INTERNAL	**INFRASTRUCTURE AS A SERVICE**	**PLATFORM AS A SERVICE**	**PLATFORM AS A SERVICE**

COMPANY MANAGES   PROVIDER MANAGES

Figure 7.7. *Distribution of responsibility for cloud computing service delivery models. For a color version of the figure, see www.iste.co.uk/helali/systems.zip*

To further explain cloud service models, an analogy called "Pizza as a Service" is often used as a tangible visual illustration.

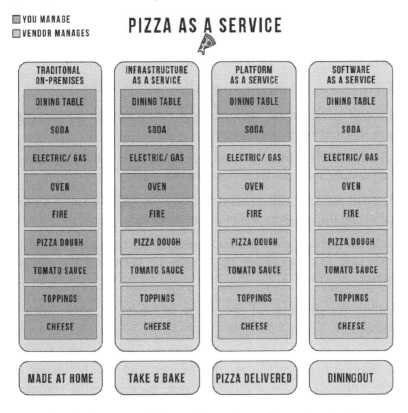

Figure 7.8. *Pizza as a Service analogy. For a color version of the figure, see www.iste.co.uk/helali/systems.zip*

7.3.4. *Types of cloud*

Two classification criteria are used to categorize the types of cloud:

– Criterion one: who manages the cloud, the cloud provider or the company?

- if the company manages the cloud with its own resources, it is an **internal cloud**,

- if the cloud provider manages the cloud with its own resources, it is an **external cloud**.

– Criterion two: who benefits from the service provided by the cloud?

- if the cloud is dedicated exclusively to the company's own needs, it is a **private cloud**,

- if the cloud is open to the public or to other companies, it is a **public cloud**.

Four typologies have been established:

– internal private cloud: the company sets up its own infrastructure and offers its services for its employees;

– external private cloud: the company operates an infrastructure rented to a cloud provider and hosts its professional services;

– internal public cloud: pertains to cloud providers. Internal services are offered within the company and to external clients;

– external public cloud: a cloud managed by third-party cloud service providers and made available to partners or clients of the company in question.

Another classification of the types of cloud is also widely used, specifically:

– public cloud: a cloud made available to the public at large. It is external to the company, accessible via the Internet and can be shared among multiple companies. An external service provider with corresponding infrastructures is responsible for managing it. The payment method is pay-as-you-go;

– private cloud: takes the form of an internal cloud structure proper to the company;

– community cloud: a particular type of private cloud that is open to partners of the company (service providers, clients, banks, etc.);

– hybrid cloud: combination of a private cloud and a public cloud that provides the benefits of both types.

7.3.5. *Areas of application*

Cloud computing is used today by both companies and private individuals. It is a technology that has rapidly become widespread and is experiencing great popularity. Several uses are currently proliferating:

– WEB2.0 applications: e-mail, web conferencing, collaborative work, CRM (Customer Relationship Management), development and testing environment;

– intelligence applications;

– simulation;

– grid computing;

– home automation;

– audiovisual media;

– automotive industry;

– industrial control of machines and procedures.

Many manufacturers and publishers have become involved in the field of cloud computing and have thus become cloud providers, such as Sun, HP, IBM, Oracle, SAP, Google, Yahoo and Amazon.

Table 7.1 shows some cloud technologies grouped according to service delivery model (SaaS, PaaS, IaaS).

Private internal	Private external	Public internal	Public external
SaaS			
Collaborative spaces	Google Apps, CRM Amazon	CMS: Content Management System	Facebook, LinkedIn
PaaS			
Web development (ViFiB)	Oracle PaaS	Free Cloud Alliance	Azure, Kawet mobile app platform
IaaS			
VMware	Virtual infrastructures OVH, Amazon	Free Cloud Alliance	Google Drive, Dropbox

Table 7.1. *Some examples of IaaS, PaaS and SaaS technologies*

7.3.6. *Advantages and limitations*

Cloud computing has numerous advantages for businesses:

– reduction of costs: usage determines costs. We only pay for what we have consumed. This approach enables a company to reduce its expenditures and to be more competitive. This automatic adaptation to demand is called *elasticity*;

– ease of deployment and innovation: elasticity enables companies to experiment and easily deploy new approaches at lower cost and with lower risk;

– contribution to Green IT by reducing electricity consumption;

– ease of collaboration: cloud computing enables a company to collaborate more efficiently with its clients and partners thanks to shared workspaces in cloud communities.

However, cloud computing is not without limitations. Some of these limitations include:

– dependence on a reliable, fast Internet connection as well as increased load on networks, which will be more heavily used;

– security issues: enormous quantities of data can be stored in a cloud provider's servers. This data, some of which is confidential, is transferred to the Internet network and can be stolen or hijacked, with potentially disastrous consequences for companies and cloud service providers;

– regulations can impose constraints, as both cloud service providers and businesses must be aware of and comply with the laws in effect, which can vary from one country to another.

7.4. Chapter summary

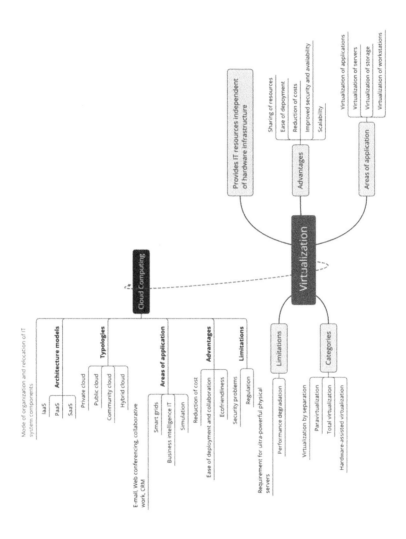

This chart is also available at www.iste.co.uk/helali/systems.zip

8

Quality of Service and High Availability

> "Quality is never accidental; it is always the result of intelligent effort."
>
> John Ruskin

– Understanding the concept of QoS and its objectives, as well as its usefulness for current IT infrastructures.

– Understanding the basic principles of QoS in networks (needs, structure, configuration options).

– Learning how to use data flow classification, improved enqueuing, and advanced load management techniques.

– Differentiating between QoS protocols or standards in the link and network layers.

– Understanding high availability mechanisms, in this case redundancy and backup.

– Describing the objectives and main protocols of level 2 and 3 redundancies.

– Understanding the general functioning of load balancing and data replication.

8.1. Introduction

These days, IT infrastructures offer more and more diverse services and serve as a framework for a wide range of applications. This varied offer must be accompanied by a service quality of assurance in order to ensure end-user satisfaction.

In reality, and in a context of convergence, services with different characteristics and different requirements must be provided by a single infrastructure that must ensure their proper functioning consistent with the levels of service required, or SLA (Service Level Agreement). Therefore, any plan to set up a network infrastructure must include and address the service quality aspect.

In the same vein, an effort to achieve high availability of the various components of the network infrastructure, mainly through redundancy, is certainly in order. This high availability helps to avoid crashes and to balance loads in order to optimize the functioning of the network infrastructure.

8.2. Quality of service

8.2.1. *Motivation*

Quality of Service (QoS) played a secondary role in the original design of the TCP/IP protocols, designed to transport data from asynchronous applications, that is, services such as file transfers, e-mail and terminal access.

However, some applications, such as VoIP and Video IP, require an adequate network QoS: controlled latencies, low jitter and low packet loss, as well as guaranteed bandwidth. This is the only way quality is guaranteed for the end-user. QoS relies on defined control mechanisms that are linked to traffic management in order to influence transport network metrics in relation to flows of information transmitted.

QoS is not a supplementary functionality like an extension for a network infrastructure, then, but the result of a large number of coordinated measures that must be anchored in the basic design of a network infrastructure. It is important to note here the interaction of the various layers of the OSI model and their requirements; indeed, it is useful to determine whether it is possible to have mechanisms in a layer that enable tolerance against malfunctions in the underlying layers.

The methods required will be discussed in this chapter. The functional elements of a network that are necessary for good QoS, and how they can be implemented with current technologies, will also be presented.

Prioritization or configuration of data traffic related to QoS, reservation of data output, limitation of data output and packet optimization are carried out by multiple mechanisms such as virtual local area networks (VLANs), DiffServ and IntServ architectures, traffic shaping, etc.

8.2.2. Definition(s)

There are various definitions of the term "Quality of Service". These include the following:

– Generic definition

"Quality in general has to do with consistency between a subject's expectations regarding the properties of an object."[1]

Quality of service (QoS) refers to the well-defined, manageable behavior of a system according to measurable parameters.

– According to Cisco

QoS refers to the capacity of a network to provide improved service for network traffic based on various underlying technologies, including Frame Relay, ATM, Ethernet, and 802.1 and SONET networks, etc.

– According to IUT-T

All of the characteristics of a telecommunications service having to do with its capacity to satisfy the stated and implicit needs of the user of the service.

– According to Wikipedia

QoS is the overall performance of a telephone or IT network, particularly as perceived by network users. To measure QoS quantitatively, various aspects of network service are often taken into account, such as error rate, bandwidth, output, transmission time, availability, jitter, etc.

QoS can thus be considered part of the characteristics of a service offered by a network. The network itself may offer various service models. It is

---

1 Quality measurement in IT networks, Razvan Beuran, 2004.

within this context that the SLA falls. The SLA is contractually defined between the service provider and the client for a specific application based on the service models offered.

Thus, QoS is an important means of assessing and judging the usefulness and above all the performance of teleinformatic networks and their services.

8.2.3. *Objectives of QoS*

QoS is principally aimed at remedying problems of network congestion or saturation, which cause latencies and data loss. It also enables the optimal support of multimedia applications, which are based on the principle of real time. Transactional applications require reasonable response time and can therefore benefit from QoS. In fact, QoS abandons the principle of flow neutrality, according to which all frames (layer 2) and packets (layer 3) are processed according to the "first come, first served" principle, or "FIFO" in switches and routers.

QoS functionality also makes it possible to achieve the following objectives:

– ensuring a certain level of quality for one or more services (the VoIP service, for example);

– isolating/protecting a specific flow from other flows;

– controlling the distribution of network resources.

The two main approaches used to achieve these objectives are:

– oversizing the network by providing a greater bandwidth in order to deal with peak traffic times. However, this solution is not economically viable, and involves poor management of resources. This is in addition to the fact that a network's capacity cannot be infinite;

– developing methods to distinguish between different traffic flows in order to classify them according to their bandwidth requirements and prioritize them according to their criticality. In sum, the goal is to manage network resources intelligently.

8.2.4. Metrics of QoS

In order to evaluate or measure QoS as well as the impact of the various underlying mechanisms, we use quantifiable parameters that characterize any data flow, specifically bandwidth, latency, jitter and packet loss, as recapitulated in Table 8.1.

Parameter	Definition	Example
Bandwidth	End-to-end output available on the network, which is the total number of IP packets successfully transferred in a given period of time.	2 Mbps
Latency	The time necessary for a packet to traverse the network from end to end, from the transmitter to the receiver, on a given support.	100 ms
Jitter	Variation in end-to-end transit time between two consecutive packets.	If the transit time varies between 80 and 120 ms, jitter is 40 ms.
Packet loss	The ratio of the number of packets lost to the number of packets transmitted during transmission.	1%

Table 8.1. QoS parameters

Each type of traffic requires a specific cluster of parameters.

Traffic type	Required parameter cluster
VoIP	Output = 64 kbps Latency <= 150 ms (to be verified) Jitter <= 30 ms Loss rate = 1%
Video, video conferencing, streaming	Output = From 384 kbps to more than 20Mbps Latency = 200 to 400 ms Jitter = 30–50 ms Loss rate = 0.1–1%

Table 8.2. QoS parameters for voice and video

In addition to the parameters cited above, which present measurable and quantifiable parameters, an assessment of QoS as perceived by the user can be useful. Thus, the QoS of a voice communication can be assessed through an MOS (Mean Opinion Score). MOS value ranges from 1 (unacceptable) to 5 (excellent) and is obtained from subjective test results.

8.2.5. *General principles of QoS*

QoS parameters are dependent on connection capacity and dynamic queuing management within switch nodes (or routers). If the network shows an overload, taking into consideration the fact that each type of traffic has different requirements in terms of QoS parameters, a queue for each class of traffic is required. The routers involved in a network implementing QoS must provide packet classification functions in sufficient queues, management of packets placed in the same queue and scheduling to control sharing of the finite capacity of the link among multiple traffics of different types.

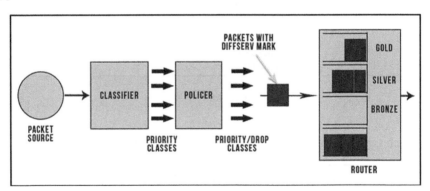

Figure 8.1. *General principles of QoS establishment. For a color version of the figure, see www.iste.co.uk/helali/systems.zip*

8.2.5.1. *Classification*

Classification is the first stage of QoS implementation. The principle consists of analyzing a packet to determine the corresponding flow, thus determining the appropriate level of service. The classification function is carried out by a flow or packet classifier based on specific classification rules. These rules may refer to headers or tagging, ports, source and destination addresses, etc. This stage is of vital importance, as it enables packet differentiation.

The packet tagging mechanism enables routers to distinguish between the different classes of data flows so that the equipment crossed is not forced to reclassify the packets received each time.

8.2.5.2. *Queuing management*

Queues serve mainly to manage congestion in a network infrastructure. A corresponding queue is created for each tag or class.

Managing these queues involves mechanisms to manage buffers, a resource limited at the switch or router level. The objective is to control the number of packets in a queue by deciding which packets to reject in the event of congestion. This means it is a packet loss control function. There are multiple techniques corresponding to this, including last-packet rejection and random early detection (RED), in which packets are randomly rejected before the queue reaches a predefined threshold. An improved variant of RED, weighted random early detection (WRED), has been developed by Cisco, which defines multiple thresholds according to traffic class.

8.2.5.3. *Scheduling*

Scheduling involves determining packet processing order at the router output level. This decision, based initially on the principle of equity, can favor certain flows to the detriment of others (real-time applications, certain protocols, specific machine source, etc.). This functionality has a significant effect on delay and output parameters for each flow. In this way, the scheduler controls the access of service classes to a limited network resource, namely bandwidth. Several scheduling techniques or algorithms can be applied, including but not limited to:

– strict priority: a priority n queue is fully processed before moving to priority n-1 queue;

– round robin priority: the router processes a packet from each queue beginning with the highest-priority queue;

– weighted priority or weight fair queuing (WFQ), in which each output queue receives a certain weighting. The available bandwidth is then shared among the different flows according to the weighting assigned.

8.2.5.4. *Traffic policing/shaping*

These are mechanisms to shape and regulate traffic, thus making it possible to control the output or bandwidth of each traffic segment in order to reduce traffic burstiness.

Traffic shaping, an operation carried out at input or within a network, ensures that traffic remains within a limit value. It helps to avoid peaks and provides a quasi-constant flow. Excessive traffic is placed in a buffer and released when possible.

Traffic policing at network input processes traffic that exceeds limits in a different way; it generally eliminates or (re)tags these packets without introducing latency into the network.

Implementing QoS in an IT infrastructure requires a preparatory phase that consists of:

– identifying types of traffic in the infrastructure and their requirements;

– determining the importance of each type of traffic for optimal company activity;

– classifying traffic;

– defining the policy to be applied to each class (minimal guaranteed bandwidth, maximum bandwidth, fixed priority level);

– defining the QoS mechanisms to be adopted to manage congestion (policing, shaping).

8.2.6. *QoS mechanisms*

QoS is a key factor for managing multimedia applications and for the success of the IP protocol as a basic unifying protocol for next-generation convergent networks. To that end, various solutions or mechanisms have been proposed to differentiate among network flows and process them adequately.

These mechanisms are based on two main approaches:

– either adapting application flows to network capacity; or

– adapting the network to application flows by managing flows via one or more resources by grouping them by class.

8.2.6.1. *In the transport layer*

At this level, RTP and RTCP protocols are implemented to manage real-time applications such as VoIP and streaming. They represent a concretization of the first approach. In other words, they make it possible to adapt the flow of an application to the bandwidth available from the network:

– data transmission in RTP (Real-Time Protocol) packets. RTP makes it possible to number packets, thus enabling the detection of lost packets, media synchronization and identification of a message's content for possible recovery in case of loss. RTP transports user data;

– quality control of the session (output, packet loss, jitter, latency) is managed by RTCP (Real-Time Control Protocol) packets. This protocol is used by receivers to send a report containing the main service quality parameters to transmitters. This information enables the source to adapt to the situation. In this way, the RTCP transports supervision packets, enabling network nodes to better control real-time applications.

8.2.6.2. *In the network layer*

This involves adapting the network to the characteristics of application flows by managing individual flows or groups of classified flows. The IETF has released both a best effort model for this and two network layer QoS management models.

IntServ

IntServ processes each flow separately from the others. To do this, it uses a specific signaling protocol called RSVP (Resource ReSerVation Protocol).

RSVP (Resource Reservation Protocol) is used to reserve resources. It is used by hosts requiring well-defined QoS for specific flows as well as the routers located along the path of these flows. Memory resources on the crossed routers are reserved by the source via signaling messages. QoS modification is possible following a request by the receiver. QoS is not integrated into each packet, but is negotiated with network equipment; this is what we refer to as end-to-end QoS. RSVP is a signaling or control protocol and does not transport user data.

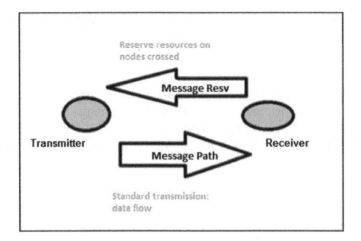

Figure 8.2. *Basic principles of RSVP. For a color version of the figure, see www.iste.co.uk/helali/systems.zip*

This IntServmodel ensures fine granularity and isolates each flow from the others. However, it is relatively complex and costly. It also comes with problems of scalability (resizing to a large scale). It can be deployed on intranets (LANs) but would be difficult to use on the scale of a service provider, for example.

DiffServ

DiffServ is based on differentiating between packets according to their class. QoS is managed by class and represents an aggregation of multiple flows. Thus, multiple classes with different qualities of service are defined by means of packet tagging from the source. Once a packet has been classified and tagged by the switch or router, a type of processing called per-hop behavior (PHB) is applied to it. PHB identifies the processing of a packet at each hop all along the path from the source to the destination. Three types of PHB are currently used:

– PHB by default, which corresponds to the best effort model;

– EF (Expedited Forwarding), which ensures that each node configured with DiffServ guarantees minimum values for latency, jitter and packet loss. This guarantee is necessary for real-time applications such as voice and video;

– AF (Assured Forwarding) provides lower quality levels than EF and is suitable for non-real-time applications.

Tagging consists of modifying the headers of IPv4 packets entering the TOS (Type of Service) field, replaced later by the DSCP (Differentiated Service Code Point) field as shown in Figure 8.3, as well as the headers of IPv6 packets and, more specifically, the traffic class field (see Figure 8.4).

Version (4 bits)	Header length (4 bits)	Service type TOS or DSCP (8 bits)	Total length (16 bits)
Identification (16 bits)		Flag (3 bits)	Offset Fragment (13 bits)
Lifespan (8 bits)	Protocol (8 bits)	Checksum (16 bits)	
IP source address (32 bits)			
IP destination address (32 bits)			
Options (possible)			

Figure 8.3. *IPv4 header and TOS/DSCP fields. For a color version of the figure, see www.iste.co.uk/helali/systems.zip*

Version (4 bits)	Traffic Class (8 bits)	Flow identification label (20 bits)
Length of useful data (16 bits)	Following header (8 bits)	Hop count (8 bits)
IP source address (128 bits)		
IP destination address (128 bits)		

Figure 8.4. *IPv6 header and traffic class field. For a color version of the figure, see www.iste.co.uk/helali/systems.zip*

The TOS field (IP precedence) displays as follows.

TOS field

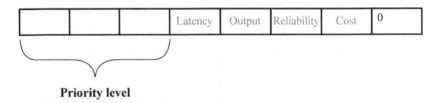

Priority level

Figure 8.5. *Structure of TOS (Type Of Service) field*

The DSCP field is coded on 6 bits and makes it possible to increase the number of priority levels compared to the TOS field, which is coded on only 3 bits.

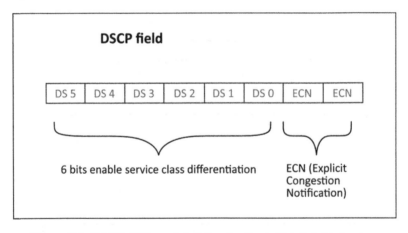

Figure 8.6. *DSCP (Differentiated Service Code Point) field structure*

The DiffServ model, by basing itself on the DSCP field, offers higher granularity, refining it by adding the 3 bits DS2, DS1 and DS0. The first three bits, DS5, DS4 and DS3, define the class called IP precedence just as they do in the TOS field. The bits DS2 and DS1 designate loss probability, while DS0 is always set at 0.

IP precedence uses the three most significant bits of DSCP, thus ensuring compatibility with the previous technique or TOS. However, it allows only eight levels of classification. Values 6 and 7 are reserved for network control and routing protocols. IP voice uses value 5, video and video conferencing value 4. The default value, or 0, is recommended for best effort traffic.

Network border routers are responsible for classifying and tagging incoming packets according to several possible criteria (header, VLAN, IP addresses, ports, ACL class-map, etc.), while routers within the network process these packets differently depending on their tag or class.

8.2.6.3. *In the data link layer*

The IEEE 802.1p method represents a QoS process defined in the IEEE 802.1Q standard. This technique uses a 3-bit subfield in the header of the Ethernet frame to assign different priority levels. 802.1p traffic priorities are thus included in VLAN tags. The objective is to differentiate between the types of traffic. Network devices compliant with the 802.1p standard can classify data traffic into priority classes. In the event of network congestion, higher priority frames are transmitted before lower priority ones.

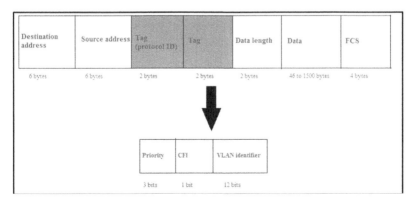

Figure 8.7. *Structure of IEEE 802.1q frame. For a color version of the figure, see www.iste.co.uk/helali/systems.zip*

With the three bits, seven classes of service are offered. These are shown in Table 8.3.

Decimal value of three bits	Priority categories
0	Best effort
1	Background
2	Reserved
3	Excellent effort
4	Streaming, multimedia
5	Interactive video
6	Voice
7	Network control reserved

Table 8.3. *Different priority categories*

QoS configuration for routers and switches is possible via several mechanisms provided by Cisco, for example:

– through the CLI command line: definition of QoS strategies at interfaces. This process is difficult to control and non-scalable;

– AutoQoS: this is a simple mechanism that ensures consistent policy application to all equipment;

– QoS Policy Manager (QPM): this mechanism implements QoS on the scale of an Internet access provider, for example;

– MQC Modular QoS CLI (Command Line Interface): this is based on modularity, and indeed QoS is constructed in blocks or modules.

8.2.6.4. *Applications*

Application 1:QoS configuration for routers

By default, routers with no QoS mechanisms process all packets in the same way, according to the first-come-first-served (FIFO) principle, but this behavior can corrupt the operation of certain types of critical traffic.

Here, we will use the MQC (*Modular QoS Command Line Interface*) approach, which has a number of advantages:

– standardization of the implementation of QoS on all Cisco platforms while masking the underlying hardware architecture. In this way, clients can upgrade to the new generation of Cisco hardware and copy existing MQC configurations;

– distinguishing between classification modifications and strategy modifications, and deactivating a QoS strategy with a single command, thanks to modular configuration. One QoS strategy can also be applied to multiple interfaces.

This approach is concretized via a three-stage process:

1) Definition of a flow class or class-map. This stage defines a set of network traffic, or a class-map in MQC terminology, using several classification criteria: protocols, access control lists (ACL). IP addresses, IP precedence, DSCP, IEEE 802.1p, etc. The class name must be specified as well as a series of match commands used to set classification criteria.

The command router(config)# class-map match-all classname stipulates that the packet must satisfy ALL criteria to belong to the class.

The command router(config)#class-map match-any classname indicates that the packet must satisfy at least one of the criteria set in order for it to belong to a class.

Once the service class has been created, we move on to specifying the criteria themselves. Table 8.4 gives a few examples of this.

Criterion	Explanation
router(config-cmap)#match input-interface interface name	The packet must come from the input interface set in order to belong to the corresponding class
router(config-cmap)#match access-group ACL number	The corresponding ACL determines whether the packet belongs to the class
router(config-cmap)#match protocol protocol name	The protocol determines whether the packet belongs to the class

Table 8.4. *Examples of classification criteria*

2) Definition of a QoS policy or policy-map in which each flow class is assigned a priority level. The definition of a policy can be used for tagging as well as bandwidth sharing. This stage represents the effective implementation of the QoS set according to the company's needs. In concrete terms, the class-map will be used to apply QoS functions such as tagging, queuing, suppression, regulation and shaping.

3) Application of the policy developed at the corresponding interface, either incoming or outgoing according to the need.

The infrastructure schema adopted for this example is given in Figure 8.8.

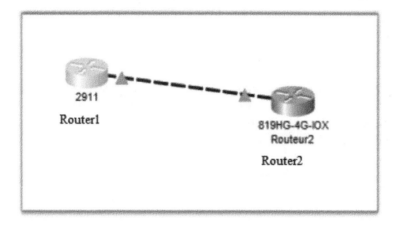

Figure 8.8. *Topology of our example*

Stage 1: creation of class-map or flow classes

The first class-map to be defined concerns VoIP traffic:

```
Router1(config)#class-map VOICE
Router1(config-cmap)#match protocol rtp audio
Router1(config) #exit
```

The second class-map defined is dedicated to web traffic:

```
Router1(config)#class-map match-any WEB
Router1(config-cmap)#match protocol http
Router1(config-cmap)#match protocol https
Router1(config) #exit
```

The third class-map to be defined pertains to FTP traffic:

```
Router1(config)#class-map match-any TRANSFER
Router1(config-cmap)#match protocol ftp
Router1(config-cmap)#match protocol tftp
Router1(config) #exit
```

The final result is recapitulated below:

Router1#show class-map
Class Map match-any class-default (id 0)
Match any
Class Map match-any TRANSFER (id 1)
Match protocol ftp
Match protocol tftp
Class Map match-all VOICE (id 2)
Match protocol rtp
Class Map match-any WEB (id 3)
Match protocol http
Match protocol https

Stage 2: creation of policy-map

A policy-map called QOSPOLICY is created using the following commands:

Router1(config)#policy-map QOSPOLICY
Router1(config-pmap)#class TRANSFER
Router1(config-pmap-c)#bandwidth percent 10
Router1(config-pmap-c)# random-detect dscp-based

A policy-map called QOSPOLICY has now been created. Next, we begin with the TRANSFER class-map. With the bandwidth command, we assign at least 10% of the available bandwidth to it. The command random-detectdscp-based, an active WRED (Weighted Random Early Detection) technique specific to queue management in a router, sets the parameters for the decision to suppress packets according to their DSCP values.

Next, we enter policy-map-class configuration mode to address the VOICE traffic class and assign its priority:

Router1(config-pmap)#class VOICE
Router1(config-pmap-c)#priority 256

This traffic class will now have a maximum bandwidth of 256 kbps but no more, and its packets will be sent before other packets.

Finally, we configure the WEB traffic class:

Router1(config-pmap)#class WEB
Router1(config-pmap-c)#bandwidth percent 60
Router1(config-pmap-c)#random-detect dscp-based

In this way, web traffic benefits from at least 60% of bandwidth, and packet suppression is based on the value of the DSCP field.

Stage 3: application of policy-map

We apply the QOSPOLICY policy at the gi0/0 interface in the output direction:

Router1(config)#interface gi0/0
Router1(config-if)#service-policy output QOSPOLICY

Application 2: QoS configuration for switches (general principles)

The implementation of QoS in this application is based on the DiffServ model, which specifies that each packet be classified upon entering the network.

Configuration commands can vary from one manufacturer to another. This configuration example is based on the Cisco Catalyst 3750 switch.

Classification, and subsequently prioritization, can be based on level 2, the IEEE.1q frame header and, more precisely, the COS field (COS values vary from 0 to 7). They can also refer to level 3, the IP packet header, and more precisely the TOS field, which can involve IP precedence or DSCP. QoS manages the use of one value or the other, as DSCP values are compatible with the previous versions of IP precedence. IP precedence values range from 0 to 7, while DSCP field values range from 0 to 63.

The class information contained in the frame or packet can be assigned by end hosts, switches or routers along the pathway, according to a configured strategy, a detailed examination of the packet, or both. A detailed examination of the packet to be carried out close to the network edge so that the switches and routers at the heart of the network are not overloaded by this task.

By default, QoS is deactivated in Cisco Catalyst 3750 switches. In other terms, incoming frames retain their original QoS tags. The switch does not modify COS or DSCP values:

Switch# show mlsqos
QoS is disabled
QoS ip packet dscp rewrite is enabled   //Traffic will be routed with
the same COS and DSCP values as at input despite this assignment

The command used to activate QoS functionality is:

Switch(config-if)#mlsqos trust [cos / device / dscp / ip-precedence]
cos   cos keyword
device   trusted device class
dscpdscp keyword
ip-precedence ip-precedence keyword

The COS value (3 802.1p priority bits) and the DSCP value of the frame entering the switch have a default value of 0. The DSCP value is calculated according to the COS–DSCP correspondence table.

Classification and tagging of incoming frames according to COS/DSCP is done in three ways: port-based configuration, MQC configuration or VLAN-based configuration. We will now discuss in detail QoS configuration at ports for a Cisco Catalyst 3750 switch.

Configuration according to ports

Configuration is based mainly on the principle of trust in the original tags of incoming frames or packets.

In the negative case, the packet will be classified using a QoS tag based on the access list (ACL) or tagging. Otherwise, there are several possibilities:

First case: in the case of an access port or a level 3 port, the command to use will be:

Switch(config-if)#mlsqos trust dscp

NOTE.– the mlsqos trust cos command cannot be applied in this case due to the lack of IEEE 802.1q or ISL tag.

Second case: involves a trunk or tagged port.

In this case, we can use one of the two following commands:

Switch(config-if)#mlsqos trust cos

or

Switch(config-if)#mlsqos trust dscp

MAP DSCP/COS table is used to calculate the value of COS if the port is configured based on the DSCP field. The MAP DSCP/COS table is also used to calculate the DSCP value if the port is configured to trust the COS.

Third case: involves a trunk or tagged port configured with the command mlsqos trust cos.

Frames coming from the native VLAN will have COS and DSCP values defined at 0. However, it is possible to configure the switch port to modify the COS value for non-tagged frames using the command:

Switch(config-if)#mlsqos cos [1..7]

With this command, the port trusts the COS values of tagged frames and defines the COS value of non-tagged frames at 0.

If the port is configured with the command:

Switch(config-if)#mlsqos cos 3 override

then the port defines the COS values of all frames (tagged or not) at 3. Previously configured trust values are thus disregarded.

Fourth case: a port in access mode to which a PC and an IP telephone are connected.

The following command is used to tell the Cisco IP telephone to tag data traffic coming from a PC connected to the same port with a predetermined class of service (COS) value. The objective of this is to prevent the PC from tagging its frames with the VLAN voice tag and thus not assigning the same priority to voice and data traffic:

Switch(config-if)#switchport priority extend cos [0..7]

It is now possible for a user to tag the PC data with a dot1q frame with a higher COS value. To avoid this situation and keep giving higher priority to voice traffic, the following command can be used:

Switch(config-if)>mlsqos trust device cisco-phone

After classification comes tagging. Mapping tables between COS and DSCP and vice versa are created with default values and then activated. For example, the following command gives the correspondence between COS values and (default) DSCP values:

Switch# shmlsqos maps cos-dscp

Cos-dscp map:
   cos: 0 1 2 3 4 5 6 7

   dscp: 0 8 16 24 32 40 48 56

The COS-DSCP correspondence table is shown in Table 8.5.

COS	DSCP (decimal)	DSCP
0	0	default
1	8	CS1
2	16	CS2
3	24	CS3
4	32	CS4
5	40	CS5
6	48	CS6
7	56	CS7

Table 8.5. *COS–DSCP correspondence table*

To manage VoIP traffic, the required DSCP value is EF (Express Forwarding), as shown in Figure 8.9 in the first line.

In our case, the port is configured to trust the COS value (mlsqos trust cos). Here, the switch calculates the DCSP value CS5 (40) to obtain COS value 5 from the COS–DSCP table. Voice traffic is thus identified by the DSCP value CS5. This is not the desired value. To obtain the DSCP value EF, we use the following command:

Switch(config)# mlsqos map cos-dscp0 8 16 24 32 46 48 56

Application Class	Media Application Examples	PHB
VoIP Telephony	Cisco IP Phone	EF
Broadcast Video	Cisco IPVS, Enterprise TV	CS5
Real-Time Interactive	Cisco TelePresence	CS4
Multimedia Conferencing	Cisco CUPC, WebEx	AF4
Multimedia Streaming	Cisco DMS, IP/TV	AF3
Network Control	EIGRP, OSPF, HSRP, IKE	CS6
Call-Signaling	SCCP, SIP, H.323	CS3
Ops/Admin/Mgmt (OAM)	SNMP, SSH, Syslog	CS2
Transactional Data	ERP Apps, CRM Apps	AF2
Bulk Data	E-mail, FTP, Backup	AF1
Best Effort	Default Class	DF
Scavenger	YouTube, Gaming, P2P	CS1

Figure 8.9. *Examples of the application and corresponding DSCP values.*
For a color version of the figure, see www.iste.co.uk/helali/systems.zip

The result is therefore

COS	DSCP (decimal)	DSCP
0	0	default
1	8	CS1
2	16	CS2
3	24	CS3
4	32	CS4
5	46	EF
6	48	CS6
7	56	CS7

Table 8.6. *Modified COS–DSCP correspondence table*

Table 8.7 recapitulates the correspondences between COS and DSCP values.

COS	DSCP(decimal)	DSCP
0	0–7	default
1	8–15	CS1 AF11 AF12 AF13
2	16–23	CS2 AF21 AF22 AF23
3	24–31	CS3 AF31 AF32 AF33
4	32–39	CS4 AF41 AF42 AF43
5	40–47	CS5 E-F
6	48–55	CS6
7	56–63	CS7

Table 8.7. *Complete COS–DSCP correspondence table*

NOTE.– All network switches must have identical correspondence tables to avoid QoS configuration problems.

Application 3: QoS configuration at a level 3 switch with VoIP management

This example of configuration gives the procedure for setting up a switch for better VoIP management based on the detection of VLAN voice and the prioritization of its flows.

There are two possible architectures. In the first, the IP telephone and the PC are connected to two separate ports. In the second architecture, they are connected to the same port.

We begin with the creation of two VLANS, voice and data, as shown below:

```
Switch(config)#vlan 10
Switch(config-vlan)#name voice
Switch(config)#vlan 20
Switch(config-vlan)#name data
```

First architecture

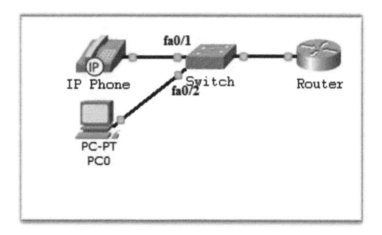

Figure 8.10. *Implementation of a VoIP solution (first architecture)*

In this case, a different configuration must be applied for the port that transports VoIP (interface fa0/1) and the port that transports normal data, fa0/2.

Second architecture

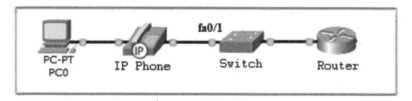

Figure 8.11. *Implementation of a VoIP solution (second architecture)*

This architecture is more advisable as it saves cabling and the application of only one configuration for a single port (fa0/1).

The CDP protocol (Cisco Discovery Protocol) is used to enable telephones to situate themselves in the right VLAN automatically.

The topology shown in Figure 8.12 encompasses both architectures.

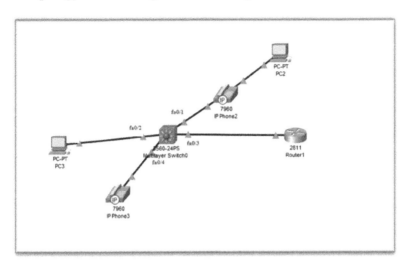

Figure 8.12. *Example of implementation of a VoIP solution*

QoS must be comprehensively implemented:

Switch(conf)#mlsqos

Next, we configure the fa0/1 interface, where first the IP telephone is connected and then the PC:

Switch(config)#interface fa0/1
Switch(config-if)#switchport mode access
Switch(config-if)#switchport access vlan 20

The priority (COS) announced by the telephone will be accepted:

Switch(config-if)#mlsqos trust cos

The following command is used to instruct the Cisco IP telephone to tag data traffic coming from a PC connected to the same port with a predetermined COS value. This is in order to prevent the PC from tagging its frames with the VLAN voice tag and thus not assigning the same priority to voice and data traffic:

Switch(config-if)#switchport priority extend cos 4

For the Fa0/4 interface, which includes an IP telephone only, we use the following commands:

```
Switch(config)#interface fa0/4
Switch(config-if)#switchport mode access
Switch(config-if)#switchport voice vlan 10
Switch(config-if)#mlsqos trust cos
```

To verify our configuration, we use the following command:

Switch#show interfaces fa0/1 switchport

Name: Fa0/1

Switchport: Enabled

Administrative Mode: static access

Operational Mode: static access

Administrative Trunking Encapsulation: dot1q

Operational Trunking Encapsulation: native

Negotiation of Trunking: Off

Access Mode VLAN: 20 (data)

Trunking Native Mode VLAN: 1 (default)

Voice VLAN: 10

Administrative private-vlan host-association: none

Administrative private-vlan mapping: none

Administrative private-vlan trunk native VLAN: none

Administrative private-vlan trunk encapsulation: dot1q

Administrative private-vlan trunk normal VLANs: none

Administrative private-vlan trunk private VLANs: none

Operational private-vlan: none

Trunking VLANs Enabled: All

Pruning VLANs Enabled: 2-1001

Capture Mode Disabled

Capture VLANs Allowed: ALL

Protected: false

Unknown unicast blocked: disabled

Unknown multicast blocked: disabled

Appliance trust: 4

Since this is a simulation with a packet tracer, verification of the prioritization of voice traffic by the IP telephone (Cisco phone) has not been successful. In fact, IP telephones do not transmit prioritized frames, as shown by the content of the frames exchanged between the IP telephone and the switch in packet tracer simulation mode in Figure 8.13. The frames preserve the default COS and DSCP values that correspond to the best effort model. This may be due to bugs in this software.

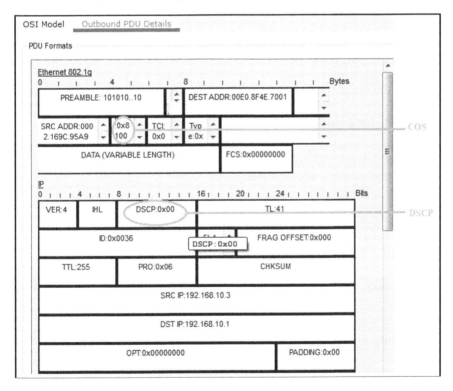

Figure 8.13. *Failure of prioritized frame transmission. For a color version of the figure, see www.iste.co.uk/helali/systems.zip*

To rectify this situation, a configuration based on the MQC approach, which consists of defining a traffic class, creating a corresponding traffic policy, and attaching it to an interface, can be applied.

Configuring flow classes

We will first define two access control lists:

```
Switch(config)# ip access-list extended voice
Switch(config-std-nacl)#permit ip 192.168.10.0 0.0.0.255 any
Switch(config-std-nacl)#ip access-list extended others
Switch(config-ext-nacl)#permit tcp any any eq 1521
Switch(config-ext-nacl)#permit tcp any any eq 1810
Switch(config-ext-nacl)#permit tcp any any eq 2481
Switch(config-ext-nacl)#permit tcp any any eq 7778
```

Next, two classes of service will be configured:

```
Switch(config)#class-map classvoice
Switch(config-cmap)#match access-group name voice
Switch(config-cmap)#exit
Switch(config)#class-map  pcs
Switch(config-cmap)#match access-group name others
```

Creating the policy to be adopted:

```
Switch(config)#policy-map test
Switch(config-pmap)#class classvoice
Switch(config-pmap-c)#set precedence 7
Switch(config-pmap-c)#exit
Switch(config-pmap)#class pcs
Switch(config-pmap-c)#set dscp af21
```

Attaching the policy created to the interface

The policy must be applied at the interface entry, in our case fa0/1 and fa0/4:

```
Switch(config)#int fa0/1
Switch(config-if)#service-policy input test
Switch(config)#int fa0/4
Switch(config-if)#service-policy input test
```

Now, the IP telephones are transmitted prioritized frames as shown by the content of the frames exchanged between the IP telephone (IP Phone 3) and the switch in packet tracer simulation mode in Figure 8.14.

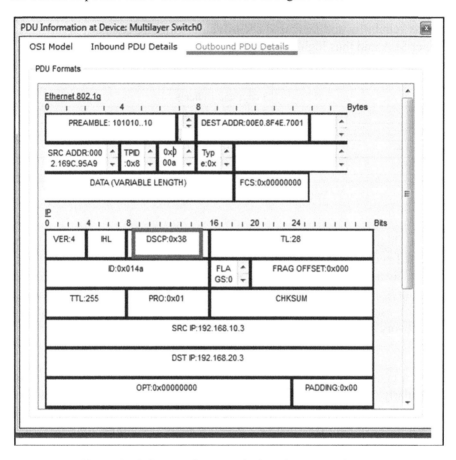

Figure 8.14. *Successful transmission of prioritized frames*

The DSCP value is equal to 0x38, which gives in decimal points the value 56. This corresponds to the class CS7 that we have defined.

8.3. High availability

High availability can be defined as a system's capacity to ensure the provision of a service during a given period.

It represents all of the methods and means that contribute to ensuring that an IT infrastructure always provides the planned functionalities and services. Redundancy, backup, data replication and load distribution help to ensure high availability of the IT system. This high availability helps to ensure greater reliability and increased security, allowing the company to provide a higher SLA and thus higher QoS.

Rate of availability	Duration of non-availability (per year)
99%	3 days and 15 hours
99.9%	8 hours and 48 minutes
99.99%	53 minutes
99.999%	5 minutes
99.9999%	32 seconds

Table 8.8. *Rates of availability in nines*

The high availability approach with its different facets should be managed and studied from the design phase onward. The implementation of highly available infrastructures requires synergy among the design, procedures and technologies deployed. In this context, certain key questions must be asked about each network infrastructure, including the parts of the network in which high availability is required, and the parts in which it is not.

As a general rule, the datacenter, server area and backbone network are particularly vital in terms of availability. New methods such as link aggregation, router redundancy protocols and load balancing enable improved availability thanks to automatic malfunction tolerance (redundancy) and the quick switching time that comes with load balancing.

Redundancy is a procedure based on the multiplication of various components of an IT infrastructure (electrical energy sources, climate-control systems, network equipment, storage solutions, etc.). The goal is to ensure that it will function in the event that one or more of these components break down, thus guaranteeing its high availability. It can be deployed in all layers of the OSI model, from the physical layer to the application layer.

8.3.1. *Redundancy in the physical layer*

This is a matter of multiplying hardware and cabling. The fact of having multiple interfaces available on a piece of equipment, such as teaming for network cards, multiple sources of electrical power, and RAID hard disks, are some examples of this.

8.3.2. *Redundancy in the data link layer*

8.3.2.1. *STP protocol*

Designed for switches and standardized with the norm IEEE802.1D, this protocol is used to determine a loop-free path in a switched and redundant physical topology, that is, with loops that cause broadcast storms. It detects and deactivates real topology loops, thus providing a logical topology in the form of a tree. If a link fails, a new path is recalculated and the network is functional again.

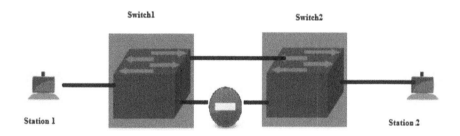

Figure 8.15. *Principle of the STP protocol*

8.3.2.2. *EtherChannel*

EtherChannel is a technology used to aggregate links or ports provided mainly by Cisco switches. It groups several physical links into a single logical link in order to improve bandwidth and to provide a level 2 redundancy mechanism. During normal operation, the load is balanced across all interfaces and, in the event of malfunction, data transport is confined to the remaining lines.

An EtherChannel link is composed of between two and eight active links which can be 100 Mbit/s, 1 Gbit/s or 10 Gbit/s, and possibly between one and eight inactive links in reserve for the event that the active links become unavailable. Indeed, theoretically, an aggregation of 4 100 Mb/s ports supplies a logical port with an output of 400 Mb/s.

The implementation of EtherChannel technology must fulfill the following conditions:

– equipment interfaces must support EtherChannel functionality;

– the same duplex mode (full duplex/half duplex) on both sides;

– the same speed on both sides;

– the same VLAN range authorized on both sides.

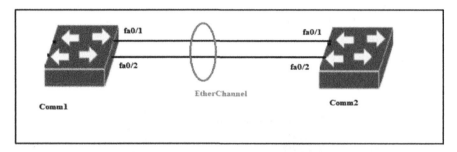

Figure 8.16. *EtherChannel operation*

EtherChannel technology is configured in two ways

The first method is purely manual; the appropriate commands must be entered on each port to be aggregated, on both sides of the link.

The second method is automatic and based on one of the two Cisco protocols: specifically, the Port Aggregation Protocol (PAgP) and the LACP protocol (Link Aggregation Control Protocol). At this stage, the existence of other protocols from other manufacturers should be indicated; in this case, Nortel MLT (Multi Link Trunking).

Example of manual configuration

The objective is to create an EtherChannel of two comm1 and comm2 switches by aggregating the two ports fa0/1 and fa0/2.

We will begin with the Comm1 switch:

Comm1(config)#interface fastethernet 0/1
Comm1(config-if)#port group 1 distribution destination
Comm1(config-if)#interface fastethernet 0/2
Comm1(config-if)#port group 1 distribution destination
Comm1(config-if)#exit

The Comm2 switch is configured as follows:

Comm2(config)#interface fastethernet 0/1
Comm2(config-if)#port group 1 distribution destination
Comm2(config-if)#interface fastethernet 0/2
Comm2(config-if)#port group 1 distribution destination
Comm2(config-if)#exit

Example of configuration with thePAgPet andLCAP protocols

The network topology is shown in Figure 8.17.

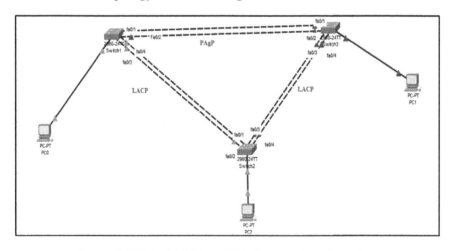

Figure 8.17. *Mock LACP and PAgP protocol configurations*

The PAgP protocol is a proprietary Cisco protocol referenced with IEEE802.3ad which offers three modes: on, desirable and auto:

– on mode activates the aggregation without using a negotiation protocol;

– desirable mode makes the aggregation request from the switch pair;

– auto mode waits for the negotiation and does not send requests, but uses the negotiation to form the aggregation.

PAgP mode	ON	DESIRABLE	AUTO
ON	✓	x	x
DESIRABLE	X	✓	✓
AUTO	X	✓	x

Table 8.9. *PAgP protocol modes*

The PAgP protocol, a level 2 redundancy protocol, is used to set up the EtherChannel technology between switch 1 and switch 3. The PAgP configuration between switch 1 and switch 3 is created using the following commands:

Switch1(config) #interface range fa0/1-2
Switch1(config-if-range)# channel-group 1 mode desirable
Switch1(config-if-range)#no shutdown

Switch3(config)#interface range fa0/1-2
Switch3(config-if-range)# channel-group 1 mode desirable
Switch3(config-if)#no shutdown

Switch1(config-if)#interface port-channel 1
Switch1(config-if)#switchport mode trunk
Switch1(config-if)#switchport trunk native vlan 99

Switch3(config)#int port-channel 1
Switch3(config-if)#switchport mode trunk
Switch3(config-if)#switchport mode native vlan 99

LACP is a standardized protocol developed by the IEEE. It functions like PAgP but supports various manufacturers. It has three configuration modes:

– ON mode serves, as in the case of PAgP, to activate the aggregation without using a negotiation protocol;

– active mode sends a request to the corresponding switch in order to create the aggregation;

– passive mode is characterized by a wait for the negotiation before switching toward aggregation. The compatibility between these different modes is shown in Table 8.10.

LACP mode	ON	ACTIVE	PASSIVE
ON	✓	x	X
ACTIVE	x	✓	✓
PASSIVE	x	✓	X

Table 8.10. *LACP protocol modes*

The LACP protocol is configured between switch 1 and switch 2 and then between switch 2 and switch 3.

We begin by configuring LACP between switch 1 and switch 2:

Switch1(config)#interface range fa0/3-4
Switch1(config-if-range)#switchport mode trunk
Switch1(config-if-range)#switchport trunk native vlan 99
Switch1(config-if-range)#channel-group 3 mode active

Switch2(config)#interface range fa0/1-2
Switch2(config-if-range)#switchport mode trunk
Switch2(config-if-range)#switchport trunk native vlan 99
Switch2(config-if-range)#channel-group 3 mode passive

Next, we configure LACP between switch 2 and switch 3:

Switch2(config)#interface range fa0/3-4
Switch2(config-if-range)#switchport mode trunk
Switch2(config-if-range)#switchport trunk native vlan 99
Switch2(config-if-range)#channel-group 3 mode active

Switch3(config)#interface range fa0/3-4
Switch3(config-if-range)#switchport mode trunk
Switch3(config-if-range)#switchport trunk native vlan 99
Switch3(config-if-range)#channel-group 3 mode passive

Verification that EtherChannel is functioning correctly is shown below:

Switch1#show etherchannel summary
Flags: D - down P - in port-channel
I - stand-alone s - suspended
H - Hot-standby (LACP only)

R - Layer3 S - Layer2
U - in use f - failed to allocate aggregator
u - unsuitable for bundling
w - waiting to be aggregated
d - default port

Number of channel-groups in use: 2
Number of aggregators: 2

Group Port-channel Protocol Ports
------+-------------+-----------+--

1 Po1(SU) PAgP Fa0/1(P) Fa0/2(P)
2 Po2(SU) LACP Fa0/3(P) Fa0/4(P)

Switch3#show etherchannel summary
Flags: D - down P - in port-channel
I - stand-alone s - suspended
H - Hot-standby (LACP only)
R - Layer3 S - Layer2
U - in use f - failed to allocate aggregator
u - unsuitable for bundling
w - waiting to be aggregated
d - default port
Number of channel-groups in use: 2
Number of aggregators: 2

Group Port-channel Protocol Ports
------+-------------+-----------+--

1 Po1(SU) PAgP Fa0/1(P) Fa0/2(P)
3 Po3(SD) LACP Fa0/3(I) Fa0/4(I)

Switch2#show etherchannel summary
Flags: D - down P - in port-channel
I - stand-alone s - suspended
H - Hot-standby (LACP only)
R - Layer3 S - Layer2
U - in use f - failed to allocate aggregator
u - unsuitable for bundling
w - waiting to be aggregated
d - default port

Number of channel-groups in use: 2

Number of aggregators: 2

Group Port-channel Protocol Ports

------+-------------+-----------+---

2 Po2(SU) LACP Fa0/1(P) Fa0/2(P)
3 Po3(SD) LACP Fa0/3(I) Fa0/4(I)

8.3.3. *Redundancy in the network layer*

To ensure high availability, individual failure points must be eliminated. Thus, a network gateway must be split at least once to prevent a gateway malfunction from making it impossible to communicate with the whole network.

8.3.3.1. *HSRP (Hot Standby Router Protocol)*

This is a proprietary Cisco protocol that offers higher availability of the network gateway. A group of routers composed of at least two routers is the foundation stone of this protocol and is identified by a number ranging from 0 to 255.

However, a single virtual IP address is assigned to all routers belonging to the group, but each one has its own priority. The election process chooses the router with the highest priority or the highest IP address as the active router. The remaining routers are now in passive or standby mode, in which they do not transmit traffic but are listening to the active router to make sure it is still operational.

This is done by means of the heartbeat mechanism, in which the active router sends hello messages every three seconds. If the other routers do not receive a hello message for 10 seconds, they initiate the process to reelect a new active router with the highest priority. This reelection process is transparent for users, who always have to communicate with a virtual router with the same IP address and the same associated MAC address, specifically 00:00:0C:07:AC:XX, in which the octet XX designates the HSRP group number.

This protocol can be configured at a router or a level 3 switch.

8.3.3.2. *VRRP (Virtual Router Redundancy Protocol)*

This protocol is very similar to the HSRP protocol and is in fact the standardized version of it. It is thus non-proprietary and compatible with other manufacturers. It uses a virtualization process to improve the default gateway availability of a local network.

A group of VRRP routers is composed of at least two routers, a master router and a backup router that share an IP address as a default gateway for members of the network. The associated MAC address is 00:00:5E:00:01:XX, where XX designates the VRID and varies from 0x01 to 0xFF. This VRID characterizes a group of VRRP routers and is the unique identifier of this group. The preemption parameter (preemp) enables the original master to take back the service of its replacement; in the event that it becomes functional again, it is activated by default. Hello messages are sent every 1 second. If, after 3 seconds, the backup routers have not received anything, they proceed with the election of a new master router.

8.3.3.3. *GLBP (Gateway Load Balancing Protocol)*

There is also a proprietary Cisco level 3 redundancy protocol based on the same basic principles as the HSRP and VRRP protocols described above. It also offers load balancing, which is fairly simple to configure.

The HSRP and VRRP protocols enable equitable load distribution via a specific configuration based on the use of several HSRP/VRRP groups with different active/master routers. For GLBP, this load distribution is based on weighting allowing for differentiated load balancing. To do this, it uses a virtual IP address associated with several virtual MAC addresses (four maximum) but belonging to the same GLBP group.

These MAC addresses have the form 00:07:B4:0X:XX:YY (in which the Xs designate the group number ranging from 1 to 1023 and the Ys represent the virtual router identifier). Grouping in this protocol is composed of two elements: the Active Virtual Gateway (AVG) router and the Active Virtual Forwarder (AVF) routers.

The elected AVG router has the highest priority or the highest IP address of the group. It replies to ARP requests generated by users, so as to distribute the load between the AVF routers based on load distribution algorithms (round robin, weighted or host dependent). It assigns virtual MAC addresses to the AVF routers and chooses from among them the standby AVC router, which replaces the AVG in the event of breakdown.

The AVF router simply forwards packets. The AVG router also forwards traffic. Hello messages are sent every 3 seconds, and the change of AVG router will take place if no hello message has been received after 10 seconds.

	HSRP	VRRP	GLBP
Ownership	Cisco proprietary	Standardized	Cisco proprietary
Roles	Active/passive	Master/backup	AVG/AVF
Virtual MAC address	00:00:0C:07:AC:XX	00:00:5E:00:01:XX	00:07:B4:0X:XX:YY
Hello time	3 s	1 s	3 s
Holding time	10 s	3 s	10 s
Load distribution	Manual (creation of HSRP groups)	Manual (creation of VRRP groups)	Dynamic and simple (load distribution algorithms)

Table 8.11. *Comparison between HSRP, VRRP and GLBP*

Application: configuration of HSRP protocol

The network topology is shown in Figure 8.18.

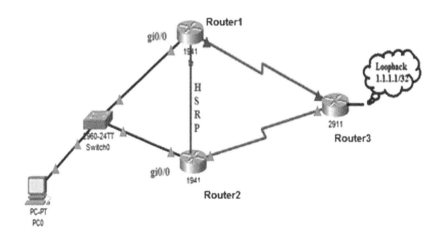

Figure 8.18. *Mock configuration of the HSRP protocol. For a color version of the figure, see www.iste.co.uk/helali/systems.zip*

Configuration of Router 1

The GigabitEthernet 0/0 interface is configured in HSRP group 1. It is assigned the virtual IP address 192.168.1.254. A priority of 250 (the highest priority is used to elect the active router) and the right of preemption is activated, that is, if Router 1 stops functioning, Router 2 takes over. If Router 1 becomes operational again, it resumes its role. In the event of non-preemption, Router 2 will retain the role of active or gateway router. The real IP address of the gi0/0 interface is 192.168.1.1:

```
Router1(config)#interface gi0/0
Router1(config-if)#standby 1 ip 192.168.1.254
Router1(config-if)#standby priority 250
Router1(config-if)#standby 1 preempt
```

Configuration of Router 2

R2 is configured with a lower priority, so preemption activation is not necessary. The interface gi0/0 is allocated the real IP address 192.168.1.2:

```
Router2(config)#interface gi0/0
Router2(config-if)# standby 1 ip 192.168.1.254
```

We have configured a loopback interface at Router 3, 1.1.1.1 /32, to simulate an Internet connection in order to test connectivity between PC0 and the loopback interface.

To verify the implementation of the level 3 redundancy protocol, the show standby command is used:

```
Router1#show standby
GigabitEthernet0/0 - Group 1
State is Active
5 state changes, last state change 00:00:32
Virtual IP address is 192.168.1.254
Active virtual MAC address is 0000.0C07.AC01
Local virtual MAC address is 0000.0C07.AC01 (v1 default)
Hello time 3 sec, hold time 10 sec
Next hello sent in 0 secs
Preemption enabled
Active router is local
Standby router is 192.168.1.2, priority 100 (expires in 7 sec)
Priority 250 (configured 250)
Group name is hsrp-Gig0/0-1 (default)
```

Router2#show standby
GigabitEthernet0/0 - Group 1
State is Standby
9 state changes, last state change 00:00:50
Virtual IP address is 192.168.1.254
Active virtual MAC address is 0000.0C07.AC01
Local virtual MAC address is 0000.0C07.AC01 (v1 default)
Hello time 3 sec, hold time 10 sec
Next hello sent in 1.163 secs
Preemption disabled
Active router is 192.168.1.1, priority 250 (expires in 8 sec)
MAC address is 0000.0C07.AC01
Standby router is local
Priority 100 (default 100)
Group name is hsrp-Gig0/0-1 (default)

The tracert command effectively tells us that the active router is indeed Router 1.

```
C:\>tracert 1.1.1.1

Tracing route to 1.1.1.1 over a maximum of 30 hops:

  1    1 ms       0 ms       0 ms     192.168.1.1
  2    1 ms       0 ms       2 ms     1.1.1.1

Trace complete.
```

We will now simulate a breakdown in Router 1 by deactivating its gi0/0 interface

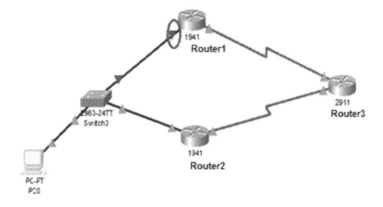

Figure 8.19. *Simulation of a Router 1 breakdown. For a color version of the figure, see www.iste.co.uk/helali/systems.zip*

The tracert command entered at PC0 effectively signals the switch toward the emergency router, in this case, Router 2.

```
C:\>tracert 1.1.1.1

Tracing route to 1.1.1.1 over a maximum of 30 hops:

  1    1 ms      0 ms      0 ms    192.168.1.2
  2    0 ms      0 ms      1 ms    1.1.1.1

Trace complete.
```

8.3.4. Redundancy in the application layer

Despite the use of redundancy in the hardware components of the network infrastructure, several factors may cause any service to become unavailable due to malfunctions in software, operating systems and applications. Thus, and in an effort to improve the overall availability of an IT system, applicative redundancy must be used for web servers, DNS servers or databases, for example.

To this end, methods have been developed such as load balancing, server switching and session switching. These are intended to relieve the burden on the server through a transparent distribution of communications over multiple computers, by subcontracting connection configuration actions and through verification of access authorization in the upstream load balancer. For example, load balancing can be used with multiple web servers which all serve the same web pages and are grouped together into a cluster. A typical configuration is the formation of a pool or cluster of servers which is addressed by the terminals using a common virtual IP address. The load balancer converts this into the real address of the real server used. Load balancing helps to improve QoS, in that it enables the regulation of traffic, thus minimizing load peaks and avoiding problems of congestion.

Load balancing is now managed by hardware solutions as well as software solutions. Microsoft's NLB, HAProxy, Safekit and Linux's virtual server are some examples of software tools.

Another possibility for the implementation of redundancy is provided by virtualization. This makes multiple virtual servers available on a single physical machine, with the result that more cost-effective and eco-friendly redundancy has become possible.

Redundancy of different services must be used according to how vital they are to the IT system.

The benefits for network operators having to do with link aggregation, router redundancy protocols and load balancing in a network structure combined with layer 2 or 3 switching can justify added costs related to additional equipment and its setup. These benefits can be broken down as follows:

– tolerance of breakdowns with simultaneous load distribution;

– transparent redundancy for terminals and servers (VRRP and HSRP);

– good scalability of capacity within a sub-network;

– rapid switching in case of error;

– creation of appropriately sized broadcast domains;

– flexible configuration of sub-networks in buildings;

– compatibility with the use of standardized protocols, particularly between servers and switches;

– possibility of future implementation of QoS functions via classification and prioritization.

Replication plays a vital role in a cluster. It ensures data consistency in redundant servers and is intended to make data secure by synchronizing it among multiple servers. DRDB, Unison and Gluster FS are examples of replication software tools.

Redundancy, load balancing, and data replication are essential means to ensure high availability in an IT infrastructure. However, they cannot provide total protection against the risk of data loss. The data which presents the real capital of each company requires the establishment of a well studied storage and backup system on remote sites.

High availability requires the incorporation of multiple technologies which must work together to make sure that the IT system's services and data are functional on a virtually continuous basis. Several high availability solutions exist in today's market; we must simply find the one(s) best suited to our situation and requirements.

8.4. Chapter summary

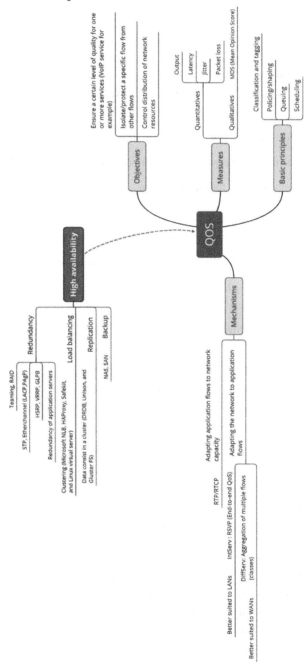

This chart is also available at www.iste.co.uk/helali/systems.zip

9

Monitoring Systems and Networks

"A house runs more smoothly when the master looks after his own
affairs."

French Proverb

- Understanding the concept of monitoring and its challenges.

- Learning the main monitoring protocols.

- Discovering proprietary and free monitoring tools.

- Taking on Nagios, the flagship free monitoring tool.

9.1. Introduction

Businesses set up fairly complex IT infrastructures in order to ensure reliable service and permanent access to data for its employees and partners.

Network infrastructures are vital to the operation of a business and its IT system, as any problem or breakdown on these networks can have harmful consequences for the company both financially and organizationally and can tarnish its brand name. In view of these facts, several parameters should be monitored, such as output, link function, cabling problems and the state of the different services in place.

To do this, rigorous follow-up and monitoring of the different components of these infrastructures is necessary to ensure that they are functioning properly and in order to intervene in the event of problems, and even to be proactive and anticipate malfunctions. This is the end goal of monitoring.

Network and service monitoring involves methods and tools that make it possible to observe everything that happens in the network and to manage its components in the event of problems, locally or remotely, in order to restore functionality. These methods include detecting breakdowns, modifying equipment parameters, measuring resource consumption, improving performance and identifying malicious activity.

9.2. Main concepts of network and service supervision

9.2.1. *Definition*

Monitoring a network infrastructure is a matter of better understanding its condition and degree of performance, verifying its proper dimensioning and the absence of overloaded links or equipment and detecting possible breakdowns. We generally monitor:

– active equipment such as routers, switches and wireless access points;

– authentication and storage servers, directories, web servers, VoIP solutions and corresponding services;

– client workstations and IT equipment in general such as laptop computers, smartphones, telephone stations and printers;

– operating systems, by measuring the use of random access memory, for example;

– applications, by monitoring the availability of application ports and processes.

9.2.2. *Challenges of monitoring*

Monitoring ensures the highest possible availability rate via the monitoring of infrastructure components, and more specifically its hotspots, in order to react quickly and appropriately to a possible breakdown. Unavailability of an IT system can cause enormous losses for the business and tarnish its image. Monitoring also enables us to prevent possible breakdowns through the rapid analysis and reporting of information in a proactive approach.

Monitoring consists of overseeing, viewing, analyzing, acting and alerting. The goal is to reduce IT-related incidents and problems to a minimum. Data collected can be aggregated into a dashboard that can aid in decision-making.

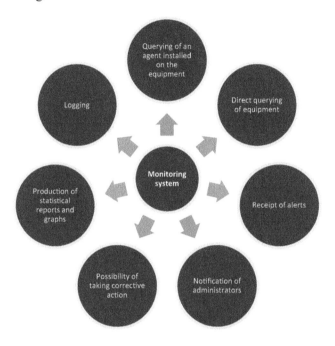

Figure 9.1. *Functionalities of a monitoring system*

9.2.3. *Typology*

Monitoring is a process that affects various levels of an IT infrastructure: interconnections (network), machines (system) and services offered (applications):

– network monitoring: the hardware concerned generally consists of switches, routers, servers (availability, probe querying, alerts), inverters, printers;

– system monitoring: involves three main system resources: processor, memory and storage;

– application monitoring: this type of monitoring tests applications hosted by servers to determine their availability, or the state of the services offered.

Methods of monitoring include:

– *ad hoc* methods such as ping, traceroute, netstat and telnet;

– methods based on network management protocols such as the Common Information Management Protocol (CMIP), which is an OSI protocol but is rarely used, and the Simple Network Management Protocol (SNMP), which is easy to implement and widely used;

– methods based on log file analysis;

– methods using local or remote commands and scripts.

Monitoring methods may also be classified according to whether they are active or passive:

– active methods are based on the sending of query and measurement requests by the monitoring platform. These are the methods most often used and are known for their reliability and the regularity of checks;

1.Request from monitoring server

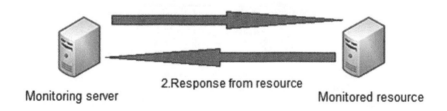

2.Response from resource

Monitoring server   Monitored resource

Figure 9.2. *Active monitoring*

– passive methods are characterized by a one-way exchange, that is, the sending of alerts by monitored resources. These methods consume fewer of the monitoring server's resources. They are also useful when monitored resources are difficult to access (proprietary hardware). However, they are not very reliable, as there is nothing to guarantee that information about the state of the resources is up to date. These methods are therefore generally used in conjunction with active methods.

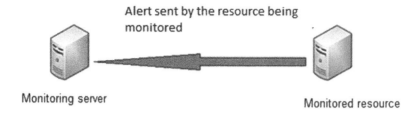

Alert sent by the resource being monitored

Monitoring server

Monitored resource

Figure 9.3. *Passive monitoring*

9.3. Monitoring protocols

9.3.1. *SNMP protocol (Simple Network Management Protocol)*

This protocol is currently the most widely used network management protocol. It is used by most of the monitoring applications currently on the market.

This protocol functions using client/server mode, which allows an administrator to retrieve information collected by network equipment only by making a request for it, or when an alert has been issued. In this way, the protocol manages networked IT equipment and diagnoses its breakdowns.

The SNMP system is made up of several elements:

– the monitoring or manager station, which carries out checking operations on the various components of IT equipment being monitored. This central station allows the administrator to monitor in real time the whole infrastructure, diagnose problems and react to resolve them;

– the network elements to be managed or monitored, which can be switches, routers, access points, servers, workstations, printers, etc. Each element has what is called an agent module, which responds to requests from the monitoring station by retrieving the management information requested, such as the condition of a port, for example. Management information data is found in a virtual database called an MIB (Management Information Base). This database is maintained by the agent and used by it to retrieve any management information it needs.

The protocol is composed of requests, responses and alerts. Requests are sent by the manager to the agent, which then sends back responses. If an abnormal event occurs on the network element being monitored, the corresponding agent sends an alert (trap) to the manager. SNMP is based on the UDP protocol. The 161 port serves the agent to receive requests from the monitoring station, while the 162 port is used by the monitoring station to collect possible requests transmitted by agents.

Types of SNMP messages	Description
Requests	The GetRequest request is used to search an agent for a variable. The GetNextRequest request is used to get the value of the next variable. The GetBulk request searches for a combined set of variables. The SetRequest request is used to change the value of a variable on an agent.
Responses	The agent always responds with GetResponse. If the requested variable is not available, GetResponse will be accompanied by the error message NoSuchObject.
Alerts	When an abnormal event occurs on the agent, this agent informs the monitoring station via a trap. Possible alerts include ColdStart, WarmStart, LinkDown, LinkUp and Authentication Failure.

Table 9.1. *Typology of SNMP messages*

The figure below illustrates the SNMP messages exchanged between the SNMP manager and agent.

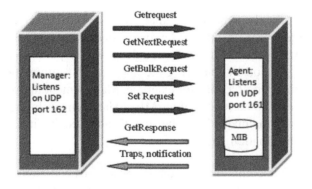

Figure 9.4. *SNMP requests, responses and alerts*

Data is organized hierarchically in an MIB (Management Information Base) maintained by the agent and queried by the monitoring station.

The MIB has a node structure in the form of a tree. Each node is characterized by a number called an OID (Object Identifier). This number is composed of one part common to all SNMP agents generally; one part common to all SNMP agents for a single type of hardware, for example, routers; and one part specific to each manufacturer, such as Cisco, for example. Each piece of hardware being monitored has its own MIB.

MIB organization is standardized according to the ASN1 standard (Abstract Syntax Number 1), which specifies a notation intended to describe data structures.

To access the desired variables, we use OID (Object Identification), which designates the placement of the variable to be consulted in the MIB. The OID is a sequence of numbers separated by the character "." (a dot or period).

EXAMPLE.– On a Cisco router, the OID 1.3.6.1.4.1.9.2.1.58 designates the utilization of the processor during the last five minutes (Object avgBusy5).

Companies active in the field are allocated OIDs by the Internet Assigned Numbers Authority (IANA).

EXAMPLE.– Cisco 1.3.6.1.4.1.9, HP 1.3.6.1.4.1.11, Novell 1.3.6.1.4.1.23.

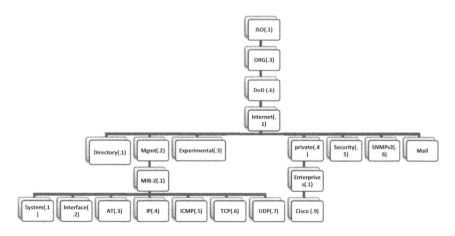

Figure 9.5. *MIB structure*

There are three major versions of the SNMP protocol:

– SNMPv1: as the first version of the network management protocol, this protocol supplies the underlying concept for the manager–agent model and the basis for communication between the management station and each agent. The only built-in security mechanism is the exchange of a so-called community string, which is sent with the respective requests;

– SNMPv2c: this offers improved security performance. Its main advantage lies, however, in recently implemented types of messages: GETBULK (to query several data items in a single request) and INFORM (for confirmations of agent responses);

– SNMPv3: the IETF has focused entirely on security in SNMPv3 and replaced the community string with a username and password. Additionally, unlike its predecessors, the third version of the protocol contains functions that can be used to encrypt the transmission of SNMP packets. Today, only version 3 is considered to meet an operable standard.

9.3.2. *WMI (Windows Management Instrumentation)*

WMI is used to monitor and manage Windows system resources. It can retrieve enormous amounts of information from a local or remote machine. Besides retrieving monitoring information, it is now possible to work on machines to install or uninstall programs, for example. An event-driven infrastructure transmits alerts according to the monitoring policy. The major disadvantage of this protocol is that it is only for Windows platforms.

9.3.3. *WS-Management (Web Services for Management)*

WS-Management is a communication protocol for the administration of servers, equipment and applications based on web services (SOAP). WS-Management is a recent protocol and thus particularly well suited for the distributed infrastructures frequently encountered these days.

9.3.4. *IPMI (Intelligent Platform Management Interface)*

IPMI provides a standardized hardware management interface. It is most frequently offered by servers (Dell, IBM, HP, Intel, NEC, etc.) and serves to manage a machine, locally or remotely, whether it is turned on or off.

It is based on a specification common to most manufacturers, consisting of a group of interfaces that make it possible to monitor a server, and more specifically, the checking of certain hardware components (temperature sensors, ventilator rotation speeds, etc.), independently of its operating system and its status (on or off) but connected to an electrical outlet.

9.3.5. *NetFlow/IPFIX*

This is a network flow monitoring program first developed by Cisco and then standardized by the IETF under the name IPFix, which is a protocol developed based on NetFlow version 9.

The collection of information pertaining to packets (source address, destination address, protocol, port) is carried out by using routers, switches or specialized network sensors. These sensors aggregate this information and send the aggregated data to a collector at regular intervals. This is a network performance management solution, offering more information and more sophisticated methods than the reference monitoring protocol, SNMP.

9.3.6. *Netconf*

Netconf was developed by the IETF as the successor to the SNMP protocol (v1, v2c, v3). It was developed to implement new-generation network management based on the language XML (Extensible Markup Language).

This protocol is based on a client–server model and allows a manager to manipulate network equipment configurations by sending them XML requests.

9.4. Monitoring tools

There are a number of tools available to monitor servers and the network. These are designed to enable the smooth operation of network infrastructures and systems by providing administrators with information on peripheral devices and systems. However, they differ from one another in terms of specific features having to do with interface, deployment architecture, etc.

The choice of a specific tool depends mainly on needs, budget, skills needed to install, operation and maintenance available to the company, and on the areas the company wishes to monitor, that is, the network, system, applications or all three at once.

Monitoring needs can in fact vary widely. Some companies wish simply to be able to view in real time the functioning of their IT infrastructure, while others also desire to be notified in the event of problems or to measure performance or statistics to aid in decision-making.

9.4.1. *Commercial monitoring solutions (HP OpenView, Tivoli) and software publisher solutions*

Aware of the importance of monitoring for companies needing high availability of their IT system and thus their IT infrastructure, major software publishers have involved themselves in the field of monitoring software. These solutions represent veritable monitoring frameworks; however, they are costly and often closed. We will now introduce two of the leading paid monitoring software programs: HP OpenView and IBM Tivoli.

9.4.1.1. *IBM Tivoli Monitoring*

This program is used to monitor IT systems (system, network, applications, hardware, etc.) and to send alerts to a monitoring console (specifically to the Tivoli Enterprise Console).

It is among the leading products in the field as it enables proactive monitoring of vital infrastructure components by rapidly detecting problems in performance and viewing performance histories and real-time performance, as well as the consolidation of monitoring and management of distributed systems and host systems by means of a single simple, customizable work console.

9.4.1.2. *HP-OpenView*

This software is used to manage and monitor network infrastructures and services. Its main benefit lies in the centralization of management information on a single station. It is meant for medium-sized and large businesses and is based on an agent deployed on hosts to collect information on operating states and services. The agent retrieves and stores monitoring information in a database called Coda, and then sends this information to the server hosting the monitoring tool and stores it in a SQL server database.

9.4.2. *Free monitoring solutions*

Alongside the paid monitoring solutions that many companies are unable to acquire, there are free monitoring tools. The functionalities they offer are undeniably less wide-ranging, but they satisfy the needs of most small and medium-sized businesses.

9.4.2.1. *Nagios*

Nagios is considered to be the benchmark for open-source monitoring solutions. This software is used to monitor systems and networks, and its reputation in the open-source world and its star status as a monitoring program are due to its modularity.

It is based on three main components: a sequencer, which is the core of the application and executes monitoring probes on the components of the IT system being monitored, the web interface used to view information concerning monitored components and plugins or probes that represent simple autonomous programs or scripts initiated by the sequencer and simply providing the result obtained to this sequencer. These plugins are not installed automatically; they must be downloaded and installed.

Plugin return code	Service state	Host state
0	OK	UP
1	WARNING	UP or DOWN/UNREACHABLE
2	CRITICAL	DOWN/UNREACHABLE
3	UNKNOWN	DOWN/UNREACHABLE

Table 9.2. *Plugin return codes*

Since October 2009, Nagios has been available in two versions:

– NagiosCore, which is free and is no longer being upgraded or improved. Community support is the only thing keeping this version in existence;

– Nagios XI, which is paid and offers all the latest upgrades (monitoring engine, redesign of graphic interface, etc.).

Numerous products have been introduced that are based on Nagios sources and compatible with its internal architecture model (the term "NagiosCore-compatible" is used). These include Centreon, Incinga, Shinken and others.

9.4.2.2. *Centreon*

Centreon is based on Nagios concepts. It offers a web application layer that greatly simplifies configuration and administration by allowing users to modify the Nagios configuration comprehensively from their web browser rather than manually modifying numerous files. The interface offered is also sleeker, scalable and multi-user.

Centreon uses its own MySQL databases to retrieve all Nagios service-state and performance data to process and display them in its own graphic interface. The graphics generated are constructed using RDDTools, which are databases particularly well suited to graphic construction.

Centreon has become a complete monitoring platform that has separated from Nagios and now relies on three components:

– Centreon Web, the viewing interface, which provides a methodical and precise monitoring display;

– CentreonEngine, a high-performance data collection engine based on Nagios 3 and covering a wide range of existing operating systems, servers and infrastructures;

– Centreon Broker, the event manager replacing NDOUtils, a Nagios addon used to store monitoring data in a MySQL database or a flat file.

9.4.2.3. *Shinken*

Shinken is a modified version of Nagios. It consists more precisely of a complete redesign of the Nagios core in Python based on the decoupling of the various roles of Nagios.

Its distributed architecture, unlike the monolithic architecture of Nagios (a single daemon), is composed of daemons, which work together to provide all of the functionalities offered by Nagios, specifically arbitration, reaction, scheduling, polling and receiving. This more flexible approach resolves the performance problems encountered by Nagios in monitoring large infrastructures (environments consisting of several thousand hosts and services) and also facilitates the setup of distributed, highly available monitoring architectures.

Shinken is also characterized by its abandonment of the language C in favor of the language Python [104], which is multi-platform (Windows, Linux, etc.) and independent of the operating system.

9.4.2.4. Zabbix

Zabbix is a free IT infrastructure and system monitoring application. It can be used to monitor network equipment, servers, systems, applications and software, providing both technical and application monitoring.

Its architecture is made up of three components. The first is a server representing the Zabbix application core, which centralizes data and all configuration information and alerts administrators in the event of a problem. The second component is a Web interface for viewing of the information stored in the database as well as configuring the objects being monitored. The third component consists of Zabbix agents, which should optionally be installed on each piece of equipment and which operate in the background and communicate regularly with the Zabbix server.

9.4.2.5. FAN (FullyAutomatedNagios)

This is a Linux distribution that enables the quick and easy installation of all tools in the Nagios community. It also encompasses Nagios and its plugins, Centreon and Nagvis.

FAN also makes it possible to set up a complete monitoring server very quickly without having to worry about its configuration. All that is needed for this is to download and install the ISO image.

This monitoring solution is appealing to beginners, but it has some disadvantages; the version of Nagios is in fact patched, which makes it impossible to update Nagios without a new version of FAN.

9.4.2.6. *EyesOfNetwork (E.O.N.)*

EyesOfNetwork is an open-source solution that includes an operating system as well as a group of monitoring applications. It is based on Nagios and provides a complete monitoring solution on a GNU/Linux CentOS distribution. This open-source system and network monitoring solution draws on ITIL processes and enables their application technologically.

Some applications used for monitoring are listed in the table below.

Application	Role
Nagios	Used to monitor IT systems and to manage incidents and problems
Thruk	Multi-backend monitoring interface
GED (Generic Event Dispatcher)	Enables secure multi-site event management
Nagiosbp	Used to manage application criticality
Nagvis	Used to create customized availability maps
Cacti and Pnp4Nagios	Used to manage host performance
Weathermaps	Enables the creation of a network bandwidth map
Backup Manager	Solution backup tool
Eonweb	Unified solution web interface
Ezgraph	A graphic display library
Snmptt	Translates SNMP traps

Table 9.3. *Examples of free monitoring applications*

9.5. Chapter summary

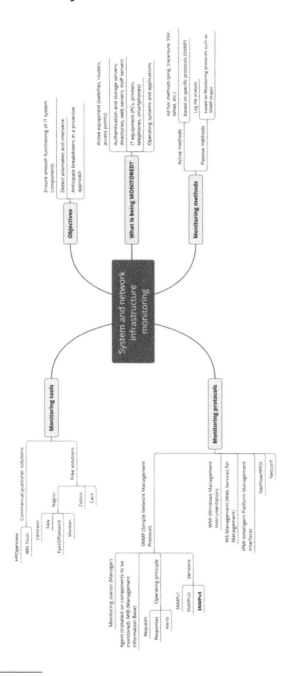

This chart is also available at www.iste.co.uk/helali/systems.zip

References

ANSII, module de cyber education (2016). *Sensibilisation et initiation à la cyber sécurité* [Online]. Available: https://www.ssi.gouv.fr/uploads/2016/05/cyberedu _module_4_cybersecurite_organisation_02_2017.pdf [Accessed November 2019].

Azrak, K. (2015). *Tutorial GNS* [Online]. Available: http://formationcisco.fr/2015/ 04/tutorial-gns3-cisco/ [Accessed June 2019].

Ben Mouloud, A. (2011). Mise en œuvre d'un système de management de la sécurité de l'information (SMSI) au sein de l'ambassade de Maroc en Tunisie. Master's thesis, Université Virtuelle de Tunis.

Bernier, F. (2013). Service DHCP. Express Edition.

Bloch, L. and Wolfhugel, C.H. (2011). *Sécurité informatique : Principes et méthodes*, 3rd edition. Eyrolles.

Bonnet, R. (2002). Virtualisation du stockage : fédérer les volumes en une unique ressource [Online]. Available: https://www.01net.com/actualites/virtualisation-du-stockage-federer-les-volumes-en-une-unique-ressource-189258.html [Accessed December 2019].

Bordage, F. (2018). 26 actions concrètes pour faire converger numérique et écologie [Online]. Available: https://www.greenit.fr/2018/03/19/26-actions-concretes-faire-converger-numerique-ecologie/ [Accessed June 2019].

Bouhet, A. (2019). Présentation du concept d'annuaire LDAP [Online]. Available: https://openclassrooms.com/fr/courses/2257706-presentation-du-concept-dannuaire-ldap/2260276-principes-et-concepts [Accessed October 2019].

Casquet, J.-F. (2004). Quels sont les outils d'aujourd'hui de supervision réseau LAN : WAN, volume 4. AZERTY MicroSystem.

Chaabani, N. (2015). Cours sécurité informatique [Online]. Available: https://www. academiepro.com/uploads/cours/2015_10_02_cours_securite_v2.pdf [Accessed November 2019].

Chapman, D. and Zwicky, E. (2002). *La sécurisation sur l'Internet-Firewalls*. French translation by Zurdel J., Editions O'Reilly.

Cisco.com (2007). Cisco Catalyst 3750 QoS configuration examples [Online]. Available: https://www.cisco.com/c/en/us/support/docs/switches/catalyst-3750-series-switches/91862-cat3750-qos-config.html [Accessed December 2019].

Conférence UIT centre média communiqué de presse (2012). La conférence RIO+20 reconnait le rôle essentiel que jouent les TIC et les réseaux large bande comme catalyseurs du développement durable [Online]. Available: http://www.itu.int/net/pressoffice/press_releases/2012/42-fr.aspx#.Xj1KiPlKjIV [Accessed June 2019].

Configrouter.com (2017). CCNP switch notes voice and video in a campus network [Online]. Available: https://www.configrouter.com/ccnp-switch-notes-voice-video-campus-network-11500/ [Accessed December 2019].

Courdier, R. (2015). ECO-TIC et développement durable [Online]. Available: http://lim.univ-reunion.fr/staff/courdier/old/cours/greenit/1_GreenIT.pdf [Accessed June 2019].

Développez.com (2010). Présentation du protocole SNMP [Online]. Available: https://ram-0000.developpez.com/tutoriels/reseau/SNMP/ [Accessed December 2019].

Di Marzo Serugendo, G. (2015). Cloud computing : architectures, services et risques [Online]. Available: https://www.ge.ch/ppdt/doc/formation/Presentation-Giovanna-Di-Marzo-Serugendo-Cloud-computing-risques.pdf [Accessed December 2019].

Dromard, D. and Seret, D. (2010). *Architecture des réseaux*. Pearson.

Fernandez-Toro, A. (2012). *Management de la sécurité de l'information*, 3rd edition. Eyrolles.

FRAMEIP.com (2019). Protocole SNMP [Online]. Available: https://www.frameip.com/snmp/ [Accessed December 2019].

Gabes, J. (2010). Shinken : quand un python rencontre un nagios [Online]. Available: https://connect.ed-diamond.com/GNU-Linux-Magazine/GLMFHS-049/Shinken-quand-un-Python-rencontre-Nagios [Accessed December 2019].

Gallon, L. (2016). Module supervision réseau [Online]. Available: http://munier.perso.univ-pau.fr/temp/ASUR4/LG%20-%20supervision/Cours-Su pervision-Reseau%20(2016)%20-%20Google%20Drive.pdf [Accessed December 2019].

Ge Jongh, S. (2013). HSRP : Hot Standby Routing Protocol [Online]. Available: https://www.ciscomadesimple.be/2013/05/25/hsrp-hot-standby-router-protocol/ [Accessed Decembre 2019].

Goffinet, F. (2020a). Blog. Fondamentaux des réseaux [Online]. Available: https://cisco.goffinet.org/ccna/fondamentaux/ [Accessed January 2020].

Goffinet F. (2020b). Blog. Principes de conception LAN [Online]. Available: https://cisco.goffinet.org/ccna/ethernet/principes-conception-lan-cisco/#1-mod% C3%A8les-de-conception [Accessed January 2020].

Guermouche, A. (2018). Administration réseau, annuaire LDAP [Online]. Available: https://docplayer.fr/16357588-Administration-reseau-annuaire-ldap.html [Accessed July 2019].

Guersen, G. (2018). Site Web GUERSEN G. *Virtualisation de postes de travail* [Online]. Available: https://www.wisper.io/fr/la-virtualisation-de-postes-de-tra vail/ [Accessed December 2019].

Henchoz, D. (2017). Le journal en ligne du Centre informatique de l'UNIL (2019). *Une infrastructure informatique plus disponible et plus verte* [Online]. Available: https://wp.unil.ch/cinn/2017/09/une-infrastructure-informatique-plus-disponible-et-plus-verte/ [Accessed June 2019].

Herve, S. (2005). Site Ingénieurs 2000. Le protocole LDAP [Online]. Available: http://www-igm.univ-mlv.fr/~dr/XPOSE2003/HERVE/ [Accessed October 2019].

IPWITHEASE.com (2017). Etherchannels modes-PAGP, LACP and on [Online]. Available: https://ipwithease.com/etherchannel-modes-pagp-lacp-and-on/ [Accessed December 2019].

Jackenod, F. (2002). *Administration des réseaux*. CampusPress.

Juganaru-Mathieu, M. (2015). Ecole Nationale Supérieure des Mines de St Etienne, cours de JUGANARU-MATHIEU M. *Cloud computing* [Online]. Available: https://www.emse.fr/~mathieu/pub/CGC/cours_CC.pdf [Accessed December 2019].

Khoudir, A. (2014). Séminaire *Virtualisation, Cloud Computing et Big Data*, [Online]. Available: https://indico.in2p3.fr/event/9743/attachments/40850/50619 /Seminaire_Virtualisation_Fev-2014.pdf [Accessed December 2019].

Khuon, T. (2015). SUPINFO, Faire du clustering avec HSRP, VRRP et GLBP sur IOS [Online]. Available: https://www.supinfo.com/articles/single/955-faire-clustering-avec-hsrp-vrrp-glbp-ios [Accessed December 2019].

Kurose, J. and Ross, K. (2005). *Analyse structurée des réseaux*, 2nd edition. Pearson Education.

La collection "Digital Studies" Fiches pratiques (2010). Qu'est ce que le Cloud computing [Online]. Available: http://www.digne.cci.fr/IMG/pdf/Fiche_16_-_Informatique-Qu_est-ce_que_le_cloud_computing.pdf [Accessed December 2019].

Laissus, F. (2009). Cours introduction à TCP/IP [Online]. Available: https://laissus.developpez.com/tutoriels/cours-introduction-tcp-ip/ [Accessed July 2019].

Léa-Linux (2002). La haute disponibilité [Online]. Available: https://lea-linux.org/documentations/La_haute_disponibilit%C3%A9 [Accessed December 2019].

Leroy, G. (2017). Gestion du déploiement d'une solution de supervision réseau multi-sites. Thesis, Conservatoire national des arts et métiers.

Longeau, T. (2016). La virtualisation des systèmes d'information [Online]. Available: http://www.alcantis.fr/index_fichiers/virtualisation_systemes_information.pdf [Accessed December 2019].

Nolot, F. (2009) Cours université de Reims Champagne-Ardenne. Modélisation hiérarchique du réseau [Online]. Available: http://cosy.univ-reims.fr/~lsteffenel/cours/Licence/Info0606/0910/Cours3-Concepts-Switching.pdf [Accessed July 2019].

Oulehri, Y. (2016). Tutoriel GNS3 [Online]. Available: https://www.supinfo.com/articles/single/3031-tutoriel-gns3 [Accessed June 2019].

Pillou, J.F. (2007). Site CommentCaMarche.net. Le protocole LDAP. [Online]. Available: https://web.maths.unsw.edu.au/~lafaye/CCM/internet/ldap.htm [Accessed October 2019].

Planet-libre.org (2009). Les différents types de virtualisation : classification [Online]. Available: http://www.planet-libre.org/index.php?post_id=1450 [Accessed December 2019].

Porte, L. (2011). Blog. Topologie réseau : le modèle hiérarchique en trois couches [Online]. Available: http://bibabox.fr/topologie-reseau-le-modele-hierarchique-en-3-couches/ [Accessed July 2019].

Pujolle, G. (2005). *Les réseaux*. Eyrolles.

Regin, J.C. (2010). Gestion de projet. Course, Université Côte d'Azur, département informatique [Online]. Available: http ://deptinfo.unice.fr/~regin/cours/cours/GestionProjet/C2_GestionProjet.pdf [Accessed June 2019].

Silanus, M. (2014). Les réseaux informatiques-Service DNS [Online]. Available: http://silanus.fr/sin/formationISN/Parcours/Reseaux/co/Reseau_web.html [Accessed October 2019].

Tanenbaum, D. and Wetherall, D. (2011). *Réseaux*, 5th edition. Nouveaux Horizons.

Tarreau, W. and Train, W. (2010). *Le Load Balancing pour les nuls*. Esceliance.

Université virtuelle Environnement et développement (2012). Le rapport Bruntland [Online]. Available: https://ressources.uved.fr/Grains_Module4/Brundtland /site/html/Brundtland/Brundtland.html [Accessed June 2019].

Volle, M. (2008). Enjeux de la sécurité des systèmes d'information [Online]. Available: http://www.volle.com/rapports/securite.htm [Accessed November 2019].

Walkowiak J. (2015). Blog Cisco Packet tracer forever, Etherchannel (LACP, PAGP) [Online]. Available: https://ciscotracer.wordpress.com/2015/10/01/etherchannel-lacp-pagp/ [Accessed December 2019].

Wallu, Pages personnelles Orange (2012). VPN MPLS [Online]. Available: https://wallu.pagesperso-orange.fr/pag-vpn.htm [Accessed November 2019].

Index

Other titles from

in

Information Systems, Web and Pervasive Computing

2020

CLIQUET Gérard, with the collaboration of BARAY Jérôme
Location-Based Marketing: Geomarketing and Geolocation

DE FRÉMINVILLE Marie
Cybersecurity and Decision Makers: Data Security and Digital Trust

GEORGE Éric
Digitalization of Society and Socio-political Issues 2: Digital, Information and Research

SEDKAOUI Soraya, KHELFAOUI Mounia
Sharing Economy and Big Data Analytics

2019

ALBAN Daniel, EYNAUD Philippe, MALAURENT Julien, RICHET Jean-Loup, VITARI Claudio
Information Systems Management: Governance, Urbanization and Alignment

AUGEY Dominique, with the collaboration of ALCARAZ Marina
Digital Information Ecosystems: Smart Press

BATTON-HUBERT Mireille, DESJARDIN Eric, PINET François
Geographic Data Imperfection 1: From Theory to Applications

CARMÈS Maryse
Digital Organizations Manufacturing: Scripts, Performativity and Semiopolitics
(Intellectual Technologies Set – Volume 5)

CARRÉ Dominique, VIDAL Geneviève
Hyperconnectivity: Economical, Social and Environmental Challenges
(Computing and Connected Society Set – Volume 3)

CHAMOUX Jean-Pierre
The Digital Era 1: Big Data Stakes

DOUAY Nicolas
Urban Planning in the Digital Age
(Intellectual Technologies Set – Volume 6)

FABRE Renaud, BENSOUSSAN Alain
The Digital Factory for Knowledge: Production and Validation of Scientific Results

GAUDIN Thierry, LACROIX Dominique, MAUREL Marie-Christine, POMEROL Jean-Charles
Life Sciences, Information Sciences

GAYARD Laurent
Darknet: Geopolitics and Uses
(Computing and Connected Society Set – Volume 2)

IAFRATE Fernando
Artificial Intelligence and Big Data: The Birth of a New Intelligence
(Advances in Information Systems Set – Volume 8)

LE DEUFF Olivier
Digital Humanities: History and Development
(Intellectual Technologies Set – Volume 4)

MANDRAN Nadine
Traceable Human Experiment Design Research: Theoretical Model and Practical Guide
(Advances in Information Systems Set – Volume 9)

PIVERT Olivier
NoSQL Data Models: Trends and Challenges

ROCHET Claude
Smart Cities: Reality or Fiction

SAUVAGNARGUES Sophie
Decision-making in Crisis Situations: Research and Innovation for Optimal Training

SEDKAOUI Soraya
Data Analytics and Big Data

SZONIECKY Samuel
Ecosystems Knowledge: Modeling and Analysis Method for Information and Communication
(Digital Tools and Uses Set – Volume 6)

2017

BOUHAÏ Nasreddine, SALEH Imad
Internet of Things: Evolutions and Innovations
(Digital Tools and Uses Set – Volume 4)

DUONG Véronique
Baidu SEO: Challenges and Intricacies of Marketing in China

LESAS Anne-Marie, MIRANDA Serge
The Art and Science of NFC Programming
(Intellectual Technologies Set – Volume 3)

LIEM André
Prospective Ergonomics
(Human-Machine Interaction Set – Volume 4)

MARSAULT Xavier
Eco-generative Design for Early Stages of Architecture
(Architecture and Computer Science Set – Volume 1)

REYES-GARCIA Everardo
The Image-Interface: Graphical Supports for Visual Information
(Digital Tools and Uses Set – Volume 3)

REYES-GARCIA Everardo, BOUHAÏ Nasreddine
Designing Interactive Hypermedia Systems
(Digital Tools and Uses Set – Volume 2)

SAÏD Karim, BAHRI KORBI Fadia
Asymmetric Alliances and Information Systems:Issues and Prospects
(Advances in Information Systems Set – Volume 7)

SZONIECKY Samuel, BOUHAÏ Nasreddine
Collective Intelligence and Digital Archives: Towards Knowledge Ecosystems
(Digital Tools and Uses Set – Volume 1)

2016

BEN CHOUIKHA Mona
Organizational Design for Knowledge Management

BERTOLO David
Interactions on Digital Tablets in the Context of 3D Geometry Learning
(Human-Machine Interaction Set – Volume 2)

BOUVARD Patricia, SUZANNE Hervé
Collective Intelligence Development in Business

EL FALLAH SEGHROUCHNI Amal, ISHIKAWA Fuyuki, HÉRAULT Laurent, TOKUDA Hideyuki
Enablers for Smart Cities

FABRE Renaud, in collaboration with MESSERSCHMIDT-MARIET Quentin, HOLVOET Margot
New Challenges for Knowledge

GAUDIELLO Ilaria, ZIBETTI Elisabetta
Learning Robotics, with Robotics, by Robotics
(Human-Machine Interaction Set – Volume 3)

HENROTIN Joseph
The Art of War in the Network Age
(Intellectual Technologies Set – Volume 1)

KITAJIMA Munéo
Memory and Action Selection in Human–Machine Interaction
(Human–Machine Interaction Set – Volume 1)

LAGRAÑA Fernando
E-mail and Behavioral Changes: Uses and Misuses of Electronic Communications

LEIGNEL Jean-Louis, UNGARO Thierry, STAAR Adrien
Digital Transformation
(Advances in Information Systems Set – Volume 6)

NOYER Jean-Max
Transformation of Collective Intelligences
(Intellectual Technologies Set – Volume 2)

VENTRE Daniel
Information Warfare – 2nd edition

VITALIS André
The Uncertain Digital Revolution
(Computing and Connected Society Set – Volume 1)

2015

ARDUIN Pierre-Emmanuel, GRUNDSTEIN Michel, ROSENTHAL-SABROUX Camille
Information and Knowledge System
(Advances in Information Systems Set – Volume 2)

BÉRANGER Jérôme
Medical Information Systems Ethics

BRONNER Gérald
Belief and Misbelief Asymmetry on the Internet

IAFRATE Fernando
From Big Data to Smart Data
(Advances in Information Systems Set – Volume 1)

KRICHEN Saoussen, BEN JOUIDA Sihem
Supply Chain Management and its Applications in Computer Science

NEGRE Elsa
Information and Recommender Systems
(Advances in Information Systems Set – Volume 4)

POMEROL Jean-Charles, EPELBOIN Yves, THOURY Claire
MOOCs

SALLES Maryse
Decision-Making and the Information System
(Advances in Information Systems Set – Volume 3)

SAMARA Tarek
ERP and Information Systems: Integration or Disintegration
(Advances in Information Systems Set – Volume 5)

2014

DINET Jérôme
Information Retrieval in Digital Environments

HÉNO Raphaële, CHANDELIER Laure
3D Modeling of Buildings: Outstanding Sites

KEMBELLEC Gérald, CHARTRON Ghislaine, SALEH Imad
Recommender Systems

MATHIAN Hélène, SANDERS Lena
Spatio-temporal Approaches: Geographic Objects and Change Process

PLANTIN Jean-Christophe
Participatory Mapping

VENTRE Daniel
Chinese Cybersecurity and Defense

2013

BERNIK Igor
Cybercrime and Cyberwarfare

CAPET Philippe, DELAVALLADE Thomas
Information Evaluation

LEBRATY Jean-Fabrice, LOBRE-LEBRATY Katia
Crowdsourcing: One Step Beyond

SALLABERRY Christian
Geographical Information Retrieval in Textual Corpora

2012

BUCHER Bénédicte, LE BER Florence
Innovative Software Development in GIS

GAUSSIER Eric, YVON François
Textual Information Access

STOCKINGER Peter
Audiovisual Archives: Digital Text and Discourse Analysis

VENTRE Daniel
Cyber Conflict

2011

BANOS Arnaud, THÉVENIN Thomas
Geographical Information and Urban Transport Systems

DAUPHINÉ André
Fractal Geography

LEMBERGER Pirmin, MOREL Mederic
Managing Complexity of Information Systems

STOCKINGER Peter
Introduction to Audiovisual Archives

STOCKINGER Peter
Digital Audiovisual Archives

ROCHE Stéphane, CARON Claude
Organizational Facets of GIS

2008

BRUGNOT Gérard
Spatial Management of Risks

FINKE Gerd
Operations Research and Networks

GUERMOND Yves
Modeling Process in Geography

KANEVSKI Michael
Advanced Mapping of Environmental Data

MANOUVRIER Bernard, LAURENT Ménard
Application Integration: EAI, B2B, BPM and SOA

PAPY Fabrice
Digital Libraries

2007

DOBESCH Hartwig, DUMOLARD Pierre, DYRAS Izabela
Spatial Interpolation for Climate Data

SANDERS Lena
Models in Spatial Analysis

2006

CLIQUET Gérard
Geomarketing

CORNIOU Jean-Pierre
Looking Back and Going Forward in IT

DEVILLERS Rodolphe, JEANSOULIN Robert
Fundamentals of Spatial Data Quality

Printed and bound by CPI Group (UK) Ltd, Croydon, CR0 4YY

27/10/2024

14580727-0001